2nd TAF Spitfire

The story of Spitfire ML 407

by **Hugh Smallwood**

Foreword by **Johnnie Houlton DFC**

2nd TAF Spitfire is dedicated to Nick Grace 1936-1988.

Acknowledgments for the Second Edition

I have set out in Appendix 4 a comprehensive list of sources, both official and private, to which I owe thanks in the writing of *"2nd TAF Spitfire"*. It has been most gratifying, and often touching, to have so much unstinting help, particularly in response to "cold" letters and phone-calls which often meant the recipient writing down memoirs or lending irreplaceable photos. To all the individuals and institutions listed under "Sources" – thanks.

I also extend my gratitude to Johnnie Houlton and his publisher John Murray for the freedom to quote from *"Spitfire Strikes"*, to Ian Mulelly for his contribution on superchargers, to James Pickering and the late Jack Thorn, for theirs on 151 RU(A) and Joe Roddis on 485 Squadron. Appreciation is also due to Carolyn Grace for information, patience and support in this project.

On the production side I would like to mention Simon Hague (design and artwork) and John Welburn Associates (photography). A special vote of thanks goes to Tom McArthur for the colour profile drawings.

Finally, apologies are due again to my wife and children, who put up with my regular disappearance from the family scene during the preparation of this edition of *"2nd TAF Spitfire"*.

H.R.S. 1994

Contents

Acknowledgments	2
Foreword	4
A Vickers Supermarine type 361 Spitfire LF Mk IXe	6
Castle Bromwich, Birthplace of ML 407	13
485 (New Zealand) Squadron	23
341 (Free French) Squadron	65
308 (Polish) Squadron	72
349 (Belgian) Squadron	78
345 (Free French) Squadron	84
332 (Norwegian) Squadron	88
Return to 485 Squadron	92
Test and Delivery Section, 151 RU(A)	94
Trainer Conversion of ML 407	104
Irish Air Corps	106
Spitfire in Limbo	114
Restoration	115
Nick and Carolyn Grace	122
Flying Colours 1944-1985	130
Appendix 1: Documents	132
Appendix 2: Operational Flights of ML 407	148
Significant quotes for ML 407 from 485 Squadron ORB	153
Appendix 3: Movement Record 1944-1994	154
Appendix 4: List of Sources	156

THE GRACE SPITFIRE ML 407

Published by Solo Enterprises

© H.R. Smallwood 1986 and 1994.

All rights reserved. No part of this publication may be reproduced, stored in a retrieval system, or transmitted, in any form or by any means, electronic, mechanical, photocopying, recording or otherwise, without the prior permission of H.R. Smallwood, Connahs Quay, Shire Lane, Chorleywood, Herts, WD3 5NU, England.

Printed in England by Wolsey Press Ltd.
ISBN 0 9511390 2 9

Designed and Produced by Kew Nim, Chorleywood, England.

This edition published 1994 by Solo Enterprises, PO Box 1174, Halstead, Essex, CO9 2QF, England.

Foreword

Johnnie Houlton and ML 407, 22nd July 1985. "OU-V for Vicki, the girl I met after returning from Malta, who all the 485 boys were a little in love with, and who became my wife".

Time continues to narrow the focus on events of World War II, including the sustained air battles of that time. Already, the brief Battle of Britain and the durable Spitfire dominate man's perception of the global air conflict which, in fact, lasted for more than five years.

As the 1944 Allied re-entry into Europe came close and after four years in the high arenas of aerial combat, many fighter squadrons moved down to the slugging ground of close support for the Allied armies. In this re-deployment, RAF Second Tactical Air Force (2nd TAF) became the hammer striking on the anvil of Second British Army, from the Normandy beaches right through to the plains of north-west Germany.

Since Dunkirk, the graceful Spitfire had maintained its lead in the air war over western Europe and now, with eminent versatility, the aircraft was to slip into its new rôle in the airborne artillery units above the front line soldiers.

As a pilot of 485 (NZ) Squadron I became the first "owner" of Spitfire ML 407 in May 1944, when ATA ferry pilot Jackie Sorour delivered her to our 135 Wing Airfield at Selsey Bill. I had flown four other Spitfires carrying the Squadron and personal insignia of "OU-V", but ML 407 was undoubtedly the best of them all and she served us well.

OU-V was one of 1,000 fighters patrolling the invasion beaches on D-Day as the armies surged ashore and in mid-afternoon, with my "Section" of New Zealanders, we accounted for the first two enemy aircraft destroyed since the landings had begun. In the hectic days that followed OU-V scored two more destroyed and another damaged, but by the end of June we were settling into our ultimate rôle of tactical strafing and dive-bombing. Perhaps it was symbolic that after the fighter sweep years at 30,000 feet, we should have this last brief period of air fighting at 10,000 feet over the beach-head, before descending to the tree tops in our fighter-bomber rôle.

Since my last operational sortie in OU-V in September 1944, over Normandy, the aircraft had existed only in the fading pages of my log book and in my memory. From Hugh Smallwood's research it is now clear that Spitfire ML 407 flew on with 2nd Tactical Air Force, right up to the end of the war.

The fact that OU-V has survived at all is but the first in a remarkable series of coincidences, which are documented in this book and in my own work *"Spitfire Strikes"*. The Spitfires still in flying condition might, at best, muster enough to put one Squadron into the air, each with its own history and roll of pilots past. ML 407 is probably the most accurately and fully documented Spitfire of this select number, which is a real tribute to the patience and persistence of Hugh in tracking down the detail recorded in his book. I am glad that he also makes mention of the wonderful ground-crew men who laboured, often in atrocious conditions, to keep the 2nd TAF aircraft at top-line readiness.

In July 1985 I was able to fly again in ML 407, in England, during filming of *"The Perfect Lady"*, the Spitfire commemorative film produced by TVS. This was a very moving experience, made even more memorable by the fact that my old aircraft again carried the markings and insignia of OU-V, precisely as they were in May of 1944.

The accolade above all goes to Nick Grace, whose dedicated vision and energy has restored ML 407 from a heap of tired and jaded parts, to her pinnacle of airborne excellence. When I was privileged to meet and fly with Nick in the rebuilt OU-V, I glimpsed the reasons behind his dedication, and on behalf of every fighter pilot I say "Thank you Nick".

Many Merlins have powered this Spitfire since 1944, but I was amazed to learn that the majority of the airframe components are original, some still carrying serial number ML 407. I have always felt that she was a lucky aircraft, so perhaps I should not be too surprised that she has remained uniquely intact.

The wartime RAF was truly cosmopolitan and I flew, at one time or another, with men from the United Kingdom, Canada, America, South Africa, Rhodesia, Nigeria, India, Argentina, Norway, Denmark, Czechoslovakia, Poland, Holland, Belgium and France – as well as with fellow New Zealanders. Another remarkable fact from the history of ML 407 is that she was flown in action only by pilots of New Zealand, French, Belgian, Polish and Norwegian Squadrons. Casualties were high in all RAF fighting commands and families from Christchurch to Chester to Copenhagen still mourn their losses.

When I travelled from New Zealand to fly again in OU-V, yet one more incredible coincidence emerged from the past. I flew my first Mk IX with the letters OU-V from Biggin Hill during the summer of 1943 and that Spitfire bore serial number MH 350. Hugh had located this aircraft in the Norwegian Air Force Museum and research shows that she also served with RAF 2nd TAF in 1944/45. Computer calculations show that the odds against survival of two personal aircraft of any one fighter pilot are around 68,000,000-to-one.

Back home, here in New Zealand, I again recall the early days of World War II when we followed the action from half a world away. This was indeed a war of basic freedoms for many people of many lands, and Spitfire ML 407 seems to be saying something right down and across the years. Arcing and echoing again through English airspace, perhaps she is a tangible reminder that Britain never really was alone.

Johnnie Houlton.

A Vickers-Supermarine Type 361 Spitfire LF Mk IXe

Comparison between Spitfire Mk V, F Mk IX and LF Mk IX with similar service load and universal wings with four .303-inch and two 20 mm guns. Based on A & AEE reports and Rolls-Royce figures, at combat rating.

Spitfire	Mk V	F Mk IX	LF Mk IX
Engine	Merlin 45	Merlin 61	Merlin 66
Type of supercharger	single-speed, single-stage	two-speed, two-stage	two-speed, two-stage
Maximum power at rated altitudes	1,235 hp at 16,000 ft	1,565 hp at 12,000 ft 1 390 hp at 24,000 ft	2,000 hp at 9,250 ft 1,860 hp at 19,000 ft
Climb to 10,000 ft	2.7 min	2.7 min	2.15 min
(% better than Mk V)			(20.37%)
Climb to 20,000 ft	6.15 min	5.6 min	4.75 min
(% better than Mk V)		(8.9%)	(22.76%)
Maximum level speed at rated altitudes	369 mph at 13,000 ft	380.5 mph at 15,400 ft 403 mph at 27,400 ft	384 mph at 10,800 ft 407 mph at 22,000 ft
Maximum service ceiling (rate of climb 100 ft/min)	36,500 ft	43,400 ft	40,300 ft

The Spitfire Mk IX

By August 1941 it was realised that the current front-line Spitfire, the Mk V, was inferior in both speed and climb performance above 31,000 feet to the Messerschmitt Bf 109F. At the same time the successor to the Bf 109, the Focke Wulf Fw 190, was already entering service on the Channel Front. By the spring of 1942 the threat posed by the Fw 190, which was both more heavily armed than the Spitfire Mk V and out-performed it in every way (except in the tightness of its turning circle), added even more urgency to Fighter Command's need for a vastly improved fighter.

Luckily, the answer was already in the pipe-line. As early as October 1939 the question of high-altitude bombing attacks, and the need for a high-altitude fighter to oppose them, had been raised at the Air Ministry. In the light of this, after the end of the Battle of Britain in late 1940, the Air Staff accepted the need for two classes of day fighter, a pressure cabin aircraft to operate from 35,000 to 45,000 feet and an un-pressurised version to fight up to 35,000 feet, with a speed of over 400 mph at 20,000–25,000 feet.

The first type would require a special engine designed for high-altitude performance and cockpit pressurisation. Already, in April 1941, Rolls-Royce were running a two-stage supercharged Merlin engine on the test-bed, aimed at installation in a pressurised Wellington bomber or a pressure-cabin Spitfire. The new engine was installed in the airframe of the old Spitfire Mk III prototype at the Rolls-Royce experimental flight unit at Hucknall and a duplicate installation was made in a Mk I to help build up flying time on the engine. When officially tested at A & AEE, Boscombe Down (Aircraft and Armament Experimental Establishment), the results were a qualified but nonetheless spectacular improvement over the Spitfire Mk V.

The new engine was designated the Merlin 61, and the enormous improvements were the results of a two-stage supercharger developed by Stanley Hooker of Rolls-Royce. The supercharger gear-change cut in automatically at predetermined altitudes by means of a barometric capsule, but could also be engaged, manually, lower down.

Production of a fighter to utilise the Merlin 61 was pushed ahead without delay, initially by converting Spitfire Mk V airframes. This involved various

Identification of the Spitfire Mk IX

This illustration depicts a "c" wing Spitfire LF Mk IX with .5-inch machine guns fitted inboard of the cannons. By summer 1944 new Spitfires with this weapon combination had a purpose-built "e" wing.

changes including strengthening of the engine mountings, new cowlings to accommodate a heavier and longer (by nine inches) power unit, stiffened rear fuselage and a considerably modified cooling system. This last change brought about the most obvious external difference from the earlier marks, with the appearance of identical-looking radiator housings under both wings. In the port housing was the oil-cooler and an engine-coolant radiator, and in the starboard housing was another engine-coolant radiator and a radiator for the new supercharger intercooler.

The engine drove a four-blade, constant speed Rotol (Rolls-Royce/Bristol, founded 1937) airscrew, with Dural, Jablo or Hydulignum blades.

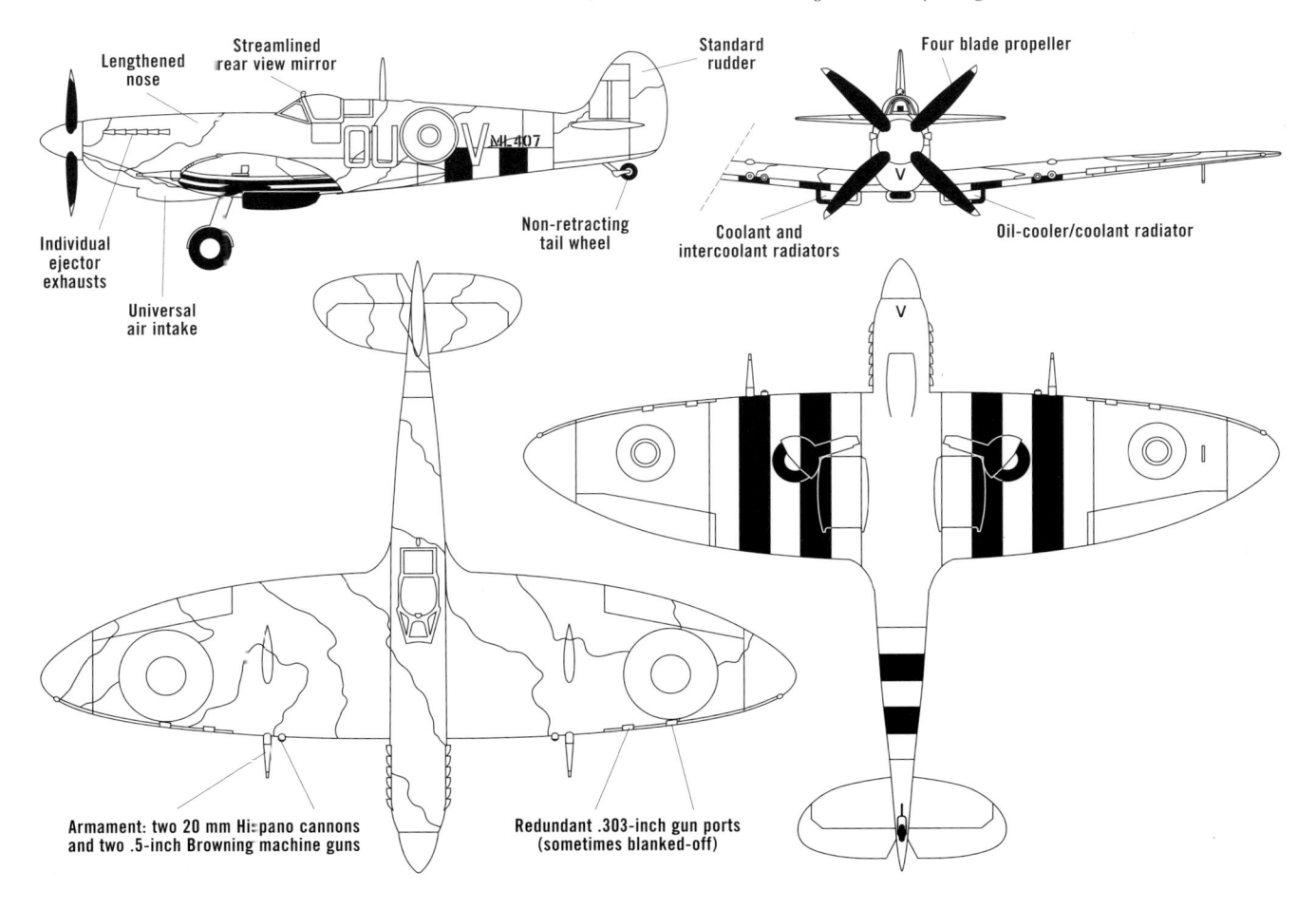

Spitfire wing armament

"a" wing

"b" wing (drum-fed Hispano)

"b" wing (belt-fed Hispano)

"c" (universal) wing

The new variant was given the type number 361, and dubbed the Spitfire Mk IX and the first were delivered in July 1942. Altogether 5,665 Mk IXs were built in a variety of versions, the majority at Vickers Armstrongs Castle Bromwich factory, only 561 being produced by Supermarine.

The Spitfire LF Mk IX

During the early war years, notably in the Battle of Britain, the emphasis in fighter development was on the search for more and more combat altitude, following the principle of whoever held the height advantage also held the fundamental tactical advantage. But during 1942 both the Luftwaffe and the RAF seemed to settle for an optimum combat altitude of between 15,000 and 25,000 feet. The Merlin 61 engine had of course been developed to provide high-altitude performance and unfortunately the parity of the Mk IX with the Fw 190 was not maintained at medium altitude. This was particularly evident in the Spitfire's inferior rate of climb.

Two measures were taken to improve the performance of the Mk IX in this all important height band. Lateral control was improved simply by removing the wing-tips (a modification not universally applied), though this resulted in increased wing-loading and span-loading and consequent aerodynamic penalties higher-up. Then an initial improvement in engine performance was achieved, by an increase in the allowable manifold-pressure for combat, from plus 12 to plus 18 psi.

However, the real solution to improved low- and medium-level performance lay in rescheduling the low and high supercharger-blower gear-ratios, which then provided the maximum effect within the required height bands. The modified engine became the Merlin 66, which came into service in early 1943 and Spitfires with this engine were given the prefix LF (for Low altitude Fighter rôle).

The Spitfire LF Mk IXe

The suffix "e" to the Spitfire's mark number denoted the wing (gun) armament of the particular aircraft.

By the summer of 1944 there were four basic wing types which provided a number of possible combinations of .303-inch or 5-inch Browning machine guns and 20 mm Hispano cannons. Although these four variants were designated "a", "b", "c" and "e", in RAF usage the suffixes were often omitted, used wrongly, ambiguously and generally mis-understood when a Spitfire type was mentioned in operational records.

The most common error concerns the suffix "b" and there are three erroneous explanations current among RAF veterans for the meaning of the letter. These are, i) the "b" means a de-rated engine for low- and medium-level operations, ii) it means a clipped-wing Spitfire and iii) it means any Spitfire sporting one cannon

"c" (universal) wing (two-cannon)

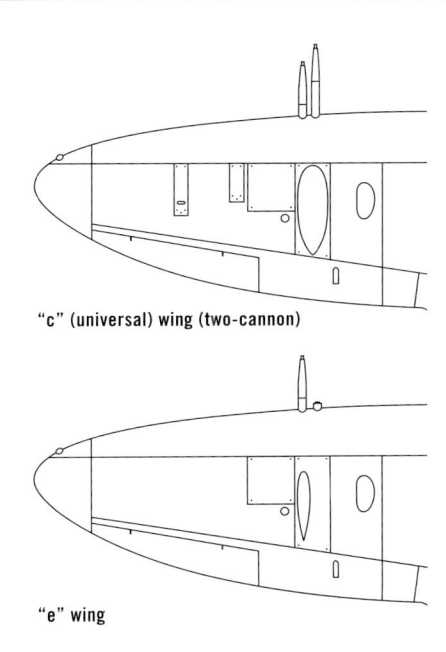

"e" wing

barrel on each wing.

In fact, when strictly applied, the suffix meant:

"a" – armament in each wing of four .303-inch machine guns.

"b" – armament in each wing of two .303-inch machine guns and one 20 mm cannon.

"c" – armament in each wing of two .303-inch machine guns and one 20 mm cannon; or two 20 mm cannons; or four .303-inch machine guns. Experimental installations were also made in this "universal" wing including three .303-inch machine guns with one 20 mm cannon and two .303-inch machine guns with two 20 mm cannons per wing.

"e" – armament in each wing of one .5-inch machine gun and one 20 mm cannon.

It is not often realised that by early 1944 a factory conversion was in existence for the fitting of a .5-inch machine gun into the inner cannon bay of the "c"-wing. This new combination, of one .5-inch machine gun and one 20 mm cannon per wing, was tested in November 1943 at A & AEE Boscombe Down.*

ML 407 was actually a "c"-wing Spitfire equipped in this way. 485 Squadron armourers remember the introduction of the .5-inch Brownings for two reasons. Firstly, because their Armaments Officer at Hornchurch devised a modification to the firing-pin (to cure a single-shot malfunction) as early as February or March 1944 and secondly, because it was presumed that the arrival of the new guns meant that the Second Front was imminent.

In any event, the factory conversion system meant that by July 25th an order could be issued that "to comply with current Air Staff requirements all aircraft issued to 132 and 135 Wings from 84 GSU (Group Support Unit) are to be fitted with .5-inch armament and Gyro Gunsights." This would include used and re-issued "c"-wing Spitfire Mk IXs.

The diagrams above show the most common of the wing-armament layouts used operationally. When .5-inch machine guns and 20 mm cannon were fitted, the .5-inch machine gun occupied the inner position which provided more ammunition in slightly longer belts, because the ammunition magazines lay outboard of the gun-bays. Another consequence of ammunition feed was the staggered breaches of the weapons, as evidenced by the "longer" inboard cannon barrel on a two-cannon "c"-wing.

---

* Johnnie Houlton and Ernie Bongard (F/Sgt Armourer) of 485 Squadron both insist that their Spitfires at Biggin Hill, in October 1943, had .5-inch machine guns. As Biggin Hill was a "crack" wing it was possible that some of its Spitfires were using the new guns well before they were generally introduced into service.

The use of superchargers in the Merlin 60 series engines.

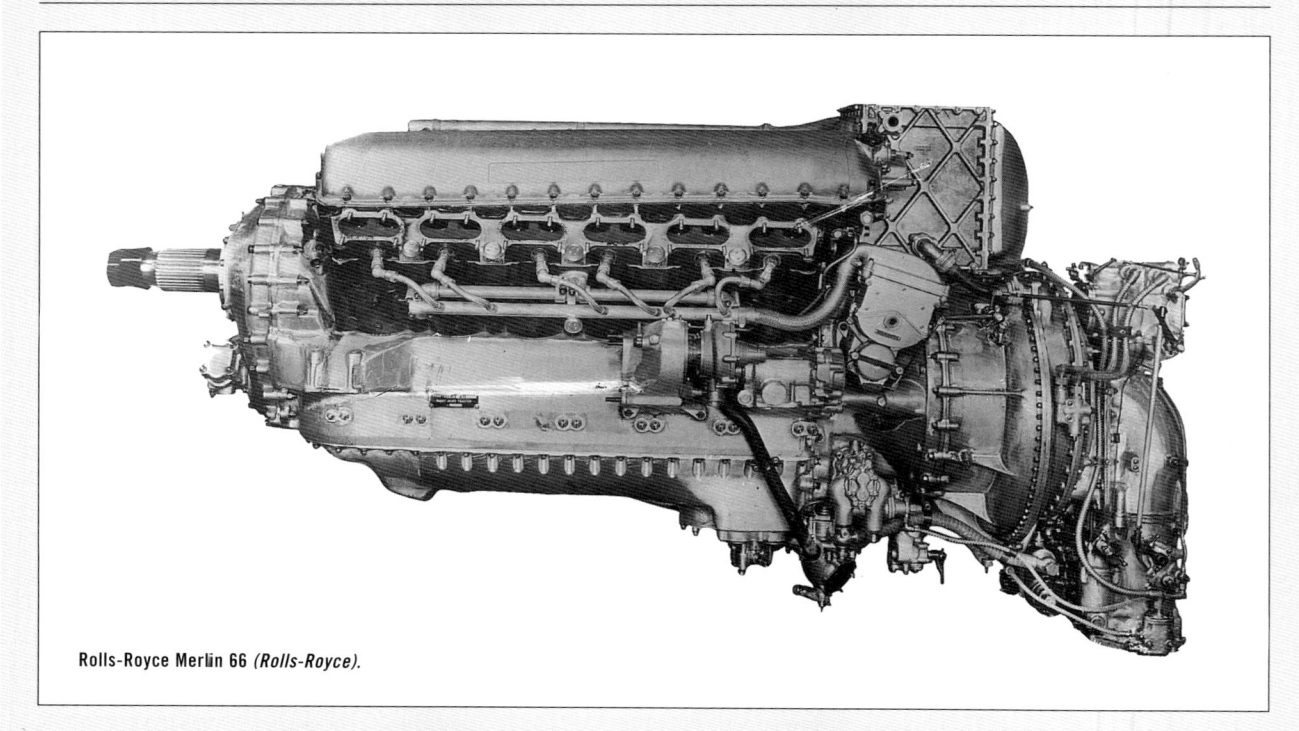

Rolls-Royce Merlin 66 *(Rolls-Royce)*.

It is possible to say that the development of the aircraft engine played a more vital part in the struggle to achieve air supremacy than any other single factor. However, the problem of performance is more complex than might first appear. Obviously an aircraft engine must be capable of producing considerable power when required, but this cannot be achieved simply by having a bigger engine, with larger or more numerous cylinders. Aerodynamic considerations aside, this would bring with it an increase in mass, which would result in a less effective acceleration, plus an increase in fuel consumption – therefore either restricting the range or further increasing the weight of the aircraft.

Supercharging

During the war, it was vital that combat aircraft should be capable of operating effectively at considerable altitude, often in excess of 30,000 feet, and this is where the big problem lay. At low-altitude it is possible to increase power by using bigger engines. But higher-up this strategy does not work, simply because the air is too thin. In very simple terms, the power developed by an engine is directly related to the mass of fuel that it burns per second. "Burning" is a process in which the hydrocarbon molecules of the fuel combine with oxygen molecules from the air. This results in the release of a large amount of energy in the form of heat, which pressurises the gases in the cylinder, which then forces down the piston. Now, roughly speaking, for every kilogram of fuel which is burnt, three kilograms of oxygen are needed, which means that about 15 kilograms of air must be acquired by the engine. In a "normally aspirated" engine this air is obtained by the "suction" created when the piston moves down on the "induction stroke". As this happens, the air is pulled through a narrowing tube in the carburettor (the venturi) where its pressure falls, so that fuel is drawn into the air-stream.

At low-altitude the air is sufficiently dense for sufficient oxygen to be obtained in this way, but at 30,000 feet the air is very thin, its density being only 1/3 of that at sea level. This means that, on each stroke of the piston, only 1/3 of the amount of air is drawn into the engine, so only 1/3 of the fuel can be burnt, resulting in a considerable loss of power. The answer to this problem is "super-charging". This can be looked at in two ways (which come to the same thing). A supercharger can be thought of either as artificially increasing the density of the air by compressing it – or as forcing more air than normal into the cylinder every time the piston moves down.

By the beginning of the 1930s, supercharging was being developed for the Schneider Trophy racing aircraft and the Rolls-Royce "R" engine had a single-stage supercharging compressor. The purpose of this was not to increase performance at altitude, as the race took place at sea level, but to get even more power out of the engine without increasing its size. The Rolls-Royce Merlin developed out of this engine and up to 1940 the single-stage compressor was adequate.

Of course, supercharging is not without its problems, the worst one being detonation, loosely referred to as "knocking". When an engine is run with a "low-octane" fuel, or on a lean mixture, or at high temperatures, or even worse a combination of all three, there is a tendency for the fuel/air mixture to ignite unevenly and/or too quickly in the cylinder. Instead of a flame spreading rapidly through the mixture from the spark plug, as is normal, a high-pressure shock wave, similar to an explosive detonation, shoots through the mixture at high speed, causing considerable forces on the piston and the rest of the engine. The potential damage from knocking is so great that it should never be allowed to happen in an aircraft engine.

In order to further "boost" performance, particularly at high altitude, in about 1940 Rolls-Royce started to develop a two-stage supercharger. As we have seen, the more the air can be compressed, the more fuel can be burnt. The compression can be increased by making the supercharger impeller rotate faster – and in order to do this a *two-speed* gear-box had already been developed. The engine rotated at about 3,000 rpm, and the impeller needed to rotate at something like 30,000 rpm, which was achieved by use of a gear-box. To give the engine a better performance at even higher altitudes, the gearing was enabled to be changed to a higher ratio when a barometric capsule detected that the aircraft had reached a certain altitude. Unfortunately there was a limit to the speed that the impeller could rotate. Quite apart from stress considerations, as the tips of the impeller approached the velocity of sound, there started to be a loss in efficiency – mainly because the behaviour of the gases changed dramatically as their velocities approached, and exceeded, the sound barrier.

Rolls-Royce overcame this limitation by using a *two-stage* compressor in the Merlin 60-series engines, and the later Merlin 70-series used the same system. This was in effect two compressors, the second one compressing the air that had already been compressed by the first one. This meant that greater compression could be obtained at lower impeller speeds.

However, higher supercharger, or boost, pressures brought with them another problem. As anyone who has ever used a bicycle pump knows, when gases are compressed suddenly they heat up. When the gases emerged from the supercharger, their temperature could have been increased by as much as 200°C (360°F). There was a danger of these gases being ignited before they reached the cylinder. But apart from this, when gases of such temperatures took part in the normal combustion process, there was a considerable danger of knocking taking place in the cylinder. These problems were overcome by the "intercooler". This was a heat exchanger placed between the supercharger and the inlet manifold, which worked in a similar way to the radiator in a car. In addition to solving the problems already mentioned, there was another benefit from having the incoming gases cooled. As they cooled they became denser, so an even greater mass of fuel-air mixture could be crammed into the cylinder. An external manifestation of the extra cooling requirements of the Merlin 60 and 70 series engines was the identical-looking radiator housings under each wing, which replaced the asymmetrical arrangement of earlier Spitfires. Inside the port housing was the oil cooler and main radiator, and the starboard housing was shared by the other main radiator and an intercooler radiator.

The problem of knocking could also be alleviated by running the aircraft on a "fuel rich" mixture. This cooled the cylinder to some extent and knocking was less likely to occur with a cooler and richer mixture. However, the biggest contribution to the anti-knocking campaign was the introduction of various additives into the fuel, mainly tetra-ethyl lead and methyl analine.

The "octane" rating for fuels is a direct measure of their anti-knocking properties, rather than the amount of energy they can release when they are burnt. Aviation fuels were given two ratings, one based on a lean mixture, the other on a rich mixture. In the early days of the war the fuel was rated at something like 91/98 octane, but later on 100/130 was developed and eventually 105/150. This meant that, as knocking was less likely to occur because of the nature of the fuel, the pressure developed by the supercharger could be increased even more.

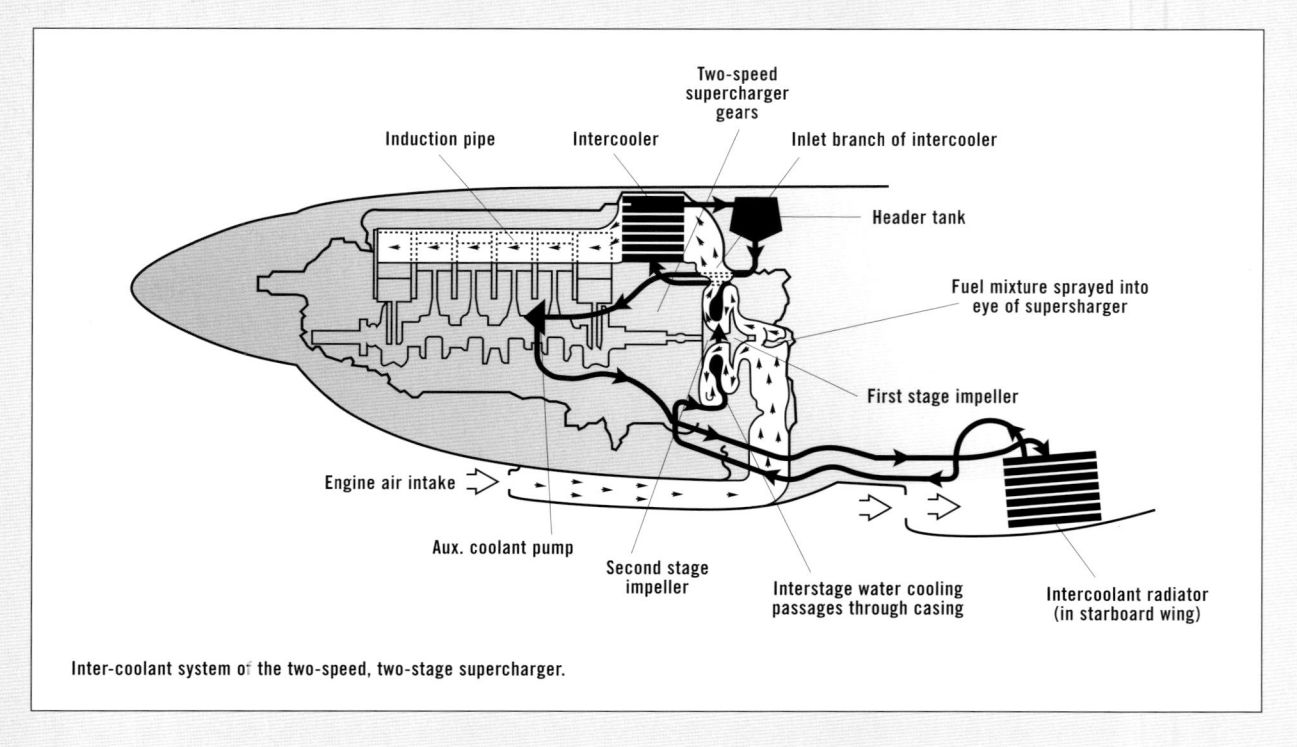

Inter-coolant system of the two-speed, two-stage supercharger.

Castle Bromwich, Birthplace of ML 407

Castle Bromwich factory from the east *(Vickers).*

The great new aircraft manufacturing plant at Castle Bromwich was built by Lord Nuffield's Morris Motors organisation as a part of the "shadow factory" system. This was first broached in March 1935 by Sir Philip Sassoon, Under Secretary of State for Air in Ramsay MacDonald's Socialist Government. By then the likelihood of war with Germany was beginning to be admitted and it was decided to draw upon the mass-production expertise of the car industry to boost the output of aeronautical equipment needed by the expanding RAF.

Among the firms chosen were Rootes Securities, Austin Motors, Daimler, Standard, Rover and Morris Motors. These companies were to provide the factories and work-force and the Government guaranteed large-scale orders. The established aircraft manufacturers were bitter that they were not considered capable of meeting the new demand, having been forced to run down their own establishments in the 1920s and early '30s in the face of successive Government disarmament and cut-back policies.

Construction of the new factory, which was to be built on a 350-acre site owned by Birmingham Corporation, was begun in 1938 and the first sod was turned in July, by Air Minister Sir Kingsley Wood. At the time, the Fairey Battle was expected to be the plant's main production model, but a switch to Spitfires was quickly decided upon.

In the event, once the building was completed and the work-force began to assemble, it did not prove so easy for the auto-motive manufacturers to turn their hands to aircraft construction. The short-term training of semi-skilled workers was a major problem. Neither were they used to the fine tolerances needed throughout production, nor the exasperating need to modify machine tools and jigs continually, often before they were installed or during a production-run.

By the summer of 1940, at the start of the Battle of Britain, not a single Spitfire had come out of Castle Bromwich, so Churchill's new and dynamic Minister of Aircraft Production, Lord Beaverbrook, put the factory swiftly into the hands of Vickers-Supermarine – and less than a month later the first Spitfire of "The Ten In June" was test-flown.

Like the parent Supermarine factory at Southampton, Castle Bromwich was an obvious target for bombing, not least because (despite its "shadow" nature) the site had been shown to *Staatsekretär* of the German Air Ministry Erhard Milch, in 1938, in order to impress him with the potential scale of British aircraft production! From the navigational point of view, the factory could scarcely be missed situated as it was on the north-east fringe of the Birmingham conurbation, with its aerodrome and the nearby cooling towers of the Hams Hall power station, which sent columns of steam far up into the atmosphere.

A wide variety of "dispersal" facilities were set up to counter the risk of a total stoppage of production should the factory be hit hard by the *Luftwaffe*. So parts for Castle Bromwich Spitfires eventually came from a carpet factory at Kidderminster, the old prison at Worcester, silk stocking and celluloid doll factories at Leicester, the Midland Red Bus Depot at Shrewsbury, Dudley Zoo and an old iron factory at Wellington.

Castle Bromwich became the bulk producer of Spitfires and by the end of November 1945, when production ceased, the factory had turned out 920 Mk II,

4,477 Mk V, 5,104 Mk IX, 1,054 Mk XVI, 122 Mk 21, 262 Mk 22 and 50 Seafire Mk 45s. The Mk IX production breakdown was 734 F Mk IX, 400 HF Mk IX, and 3,970 LF Mk IX. In June 1944 Mk IX production reached an all-time high of 320 machines in one week.

April 1944 – ML 407 Rolls Out

The construction of ML 407 took some 35,000 man hours, and the airframe (fuel tanks empty), minus the "loan embodiment" items supplied free by the Government (engine, instruments, armament, tyres, radio, etc) cost about £4,907. When complete, the Vickers-Armstrongs inspector satisfied himself that the new Spitfire was ready to be flown, then notified and submitted the inspection papers to the AID (Aeronautical Inspection Directorate) inspector, who was attached to the factory. The AID inspector then signed a "Form 1090" which certified the aircraft safe and ready to be test-flown.

Production test-flying of all Castle Bromwich Spitfires was under the control of Chief Test Pilot Alex Henshaw, a young man who had made a formidable reputation as a pre-war racing and record-breaking pilot. He led a small team of company test pilots, which was supplemented by RAF personnel as the pace of production accelerated. When ML 407 emerged from the Flight Shed, where the final preparations for flight had been made, she took her place on the huge apron of camouflaged re-inforced concrete outside, where other machines, arranged several ranks deep, also awaited their first flight.

The standard test-flight which ML 407 received had been codified by test pilots Jeffrey Quill and George Pickering in 1938 at Supermarine, Southampton, when the first production Spitfires were completed. The schedule was "fixed and mandatory" and remained intact for 10 years, with modifications and expansion to accommodate the increasing sophistication of successive marks.

"It was based on the principle that, in addition to the essential functional tests of the whole aeroplane (which were listed), the basic performance and handling should also be checked at selected points throughout the flight envelope. This meant that each aeroplane was to be climbed at maximum continuous climbing power and best climbing speed to its full throttle height of at least 18,000 feet and all instrument readings checked. This was to be followed by a two-minute level run at maximum combat power settings to check the indicated top speed and the performance of engine and supercharger. The aeroplane was then to be put into a full-power dive to its limiting indicated airspeed of 470 mph and its trim and control behaviour checked in this extreme condition. In general, and allowing for two or three short initial flights for trimming the ailerons and adjusting the engine boost and propeller settings, this schedule took about 40 minutes' flying time and

("Spitfire. A Test Pilot's Story" Jeffrey Quill — John Murray 1983)

Test pilots F/Lt Jim Rosser, Alex Henshaw, Capt Olav Ullestad and F/Lt Venda Jicha on the Flight Shed apron at Castle Bromwich, December 1943. Spitfires Mk IXc flank Lancaster Mk I, HK 535. Henshaw personally flew over 2,000 Spitfires, about 10% of the total production *(Henshaw).*

gave the aeroplane a thorough shakedown. A minimum of three take-offs and landings was also required before the aeroplane could be passed for delivery."

Such a test-flight cost the British Government £11.10s.0d.

The test-flying at Castle Bromwich was carried out in all weathers except the very worst (usually thick fog) throughout the war, without radio-navigation aids and radio. Other hazards to intensive aircraft movements were the enormous urban sprawl adjacent to the airfield, the balloon barrage over the city and the Hams Hall cooling towers – which both as an obstacle and as a source of steam could compound weather problems.

Once a Spitfire had been test-flown and was ready for collection, a pilot of the ATA (Air Transport Auxiliary) would ferry the aircraft to its first RAF unit, usually a Maintenance Unit (MU), where it would be set up as an operational weapon, final modifications and adjustments (such as harmonizing cannon) accomplished, transmitter/receiver fitted, a service test-flight completed and generally made ready for transfer to a squadron.

ML 407 Taken on Charge

About 10 days before the estimated date of dispatch, AID at Castle Bromwich applied to Headquarters 41 Group, RAF Maintenance Command, for a unit allotment. A "Form 225A" came back nominating 33 MU as ML 407's destination. 33 MU and the Ferry Pool responsible for clearing the factory (No. 6 Ferry Pilots Pool, Ratcliffe) also received a copy.

After ML 407 had completed the test-flying schedule, AID advised 41 Group and Ratcliffe and final arrangements were made by telephone between AID and the Ferry Pool Operations staff. On April 24th, a civilian ATA pilot arrived from Ratcliffe and left the top-copy of an Aircraft Collection Chit for "Spitfire ML 407" with the Flight Shed dispatch staff at Castle Bromwich airfield. They, in turn, made out a "Form 1632" and sent it to 41 Group to confirm collection. The brand-new aeroplane flew south, probably following the line of the Fosse Way, because without radio, the ATA pilots had to fly in sight of the ground and the old Roman road was a much appreciated topographical feature. Less than an hour later, the Spitfire landed at 33 MU, Lyneham, Wiltshire.

The bottom copy of the "ferry chit" having been duly signed as proof of delivery, the ATA pilot went on his or her way, perhaps taking a fully operational aircraft onward to a squadron. Meanwhile, ML 407 was left behind to have service equipment fitted and checked. The consignee advised 41 Group subsequently that the Spitfire had been received on (yet another piece of "bumph") the "Form 623". In this way, 41 Group was able to keep an up-to-date "Movement Card" (Form 78) for all aircraft as they were transferred from unit to unit, throughout their service life. ML 407 had now been "Taken On Charge" officially, by the RAF.

33 MU was typical of such Maintenance Command units, having a complement of about 16 Officers, 25 Other Ranks, and a civilian work-force of more than 700. It was a busy time for the MUs. In April, Lyneham received 117 Spitfires (of which 35 were Mk IX) and issued 106 (of which 47 were Mk IX). The three service test pilots made 388 test-flights, most of these to clear Spitfires for duty.

ATA Girl

By the 28th, ML 407 was ready to join a squadron and a signal to that effect was sent to the operations room at No. 15 Ferry Pool, Hamble, by the ATA Operations staff, Central Ferry Control, which was located at HQ 41 Group, Andover. Another "ferry chit" was made out, showing the consignee to be "485 Sq. Selsey".

In September 1941 Hamble had been taken-over by the women pilots of the ATA. "The work at Hamble consisted for the most part of short ferry trips of not more than thirty minutes' duration... Spitfires from Eastleigh, High Post and

Chattis Hill went mostly to the Maintenance Units at Colerne, Lyneham, Little Rissington and Brize Norton. The Oxfords which were destined for the North went to White Waltham as did the Walrus from the Saunders Roe factory at Cowes, unless they went to Wroughton. Because of the proximity of Hamble to the Royal Naval Air Stations at Worthy Down, Lee-on-Solent and Gosport, we used to be given for the return trip from White Waltham, a variety of Naval Aircraft of the era such as Gladiators to Gosport, Chesapeakes and Swordfish to Lee and Albacores to Worthy Down. Later there were some Blackburn Skuas and Rocs."

("The Forgotten Pilots" Lettice Curtis – 1982)

At Hamble, first thing in the morning, the business of allotting the various aircraft deliveries of the day began. Every effort was made to provide each ferry pilot with a co-ordinated schedule of deliveries to, and collections from, the same or nearby airfields – hopefully bringing her home, or to a strategically placed ATA taxi aircraft, at the end of the day.

On April 29th 1944 First Officer Jackie Sorour drew ML 407's "chit".

"The morning foretold a lovely day, as I set off on my bicycle from my billet in Hamble village, in my dark blue uniform jacket and trousers with gold rank braid and 'Wings'," she remembers. "I would try to cycle the circular mile to the airfield entrance without using the handlebars and head for the ATA Mess, waving merrily to the guard on the gates as I sailed past him.

"The plan for the day's collection and delivery of aircraft had come in overnight, and our Captain had sorted out the most economical way to save time and fuel. I collected my five 'chits' authorising me to fly five different aircraft from 'somewhere to somewhere'.

"As we could not use the radio, navigation was always by VFR (Visual Flying Rules) and at our discretion in fog or cloud. In the UK fog and cloud invariably proved a problem and we lost a number of ferry pilots due to bad weather.

"I also collected my two-ounce bar of chocolate ration, which was given to us as often we flew all day without lunch. That day I tied up my chocolate ration with a letter to my future fiancé, who was in the Army at Aylesbury. Flying low over the Army Camp in the Oxford, with flaps and undercarriage down, I dropped the parcel from the flight deck window, hoping it wouldn't hit fuselage or tail. With it was a note telling the finder to keep the chocolate, but please deliver the letter to Reg Moggridge.

"The order of deliveries that day ran, by car to Portsmouth – Airspeed Oxford R 6350, from Portsmouth to White Waltham – Hawker Typhoon R 8878, White Waltham to Eastleigh – Spitfire XIV NH 692, Eastleigh to Lyneham – Spitfire IX ML 407, Lyneham to Selsey – by car back to Hamble – Supermarine Walrus W 3062, Hamble to Wroughton – and finally back to Hamble again, flying the Fairchild taxi aircraft. I only counted actual airborne time, take-off to touch-down, so my flying

First Officer Jackie Sorour, Air Transport Auxiliary

Jackie Sorour was born in South Africa, where she was both the youngest woman to make a parachute jump and the Union's youngest woman pilot at the age of 17. A year later, in 1940, she came to Britain and as a WAAF Radio Direction Finding Operator was working at the "CH" (Chain-Home) radar station at Rye. That summer her application to join the Air Transport Auxiliary was accepted and her first ferry-flight was on July 29th.

She went on to ferry more aircraft than any other ATA pilot during the war (for which she was awarded a Commendation for Valuable Service in the Air), of which more than 300 were Spitfires. In November 1945, now Mrs Jackie Moggridge, she left ATA for the birth of her daughter, but in 1948 she joined the WRAF (Women's Royal Air Force) Reserve, where she won full RAF "Wings". Having flown jet-fighters by 1954, she was then recruited to help ferry Spitfires out to equip the Burmese Air Force. On leaving WRAF Jackie became a civil airline pilot and in 1959 was voted Woman Pilot of the Year and presented with the Jean Bird Trophy, by Lord Brabazon. Still flying, she now lives in Somerset.

Jackie Moggridge (née Sorour) in RAF uniform, while making a refuelling stop at Bahrain in 1954 with a Spitfire, en route for Burma *(Moggridge)*.

time (3 hours 20 minutes) seems short".

It was a 40-minute flight from Lyneham to Selsey, which was an Advanced Landing Ground of 84 Group, 2nd Tactical Air Force, and about seven miles south of Chichester.

The pilots of 485 Squadron found the arrival of female ferry pilots a diverting experience and food for thought when they saw the competent way they brought the Spitfires into Selsey's fairly short landing strip. Furthermore they realised that experienced ATA pilots were proficient on a much wider range of aircraft than they were. But on one occasion at least, the arrival of a Spitfire caused a mild panic. As Jackie Sorour taxied in, disguised in flying gear and helmet, she "was horrified to see naked bodies sunning themselves everywhere outside huts and tents. Every one of the nudists rushed inside when I took off my helmet and stepped out of the aircraft. I was too shy to show myself outside the office when I went to get my 'chit' signed, so waited until the taxi arrived, dashing out quickly and hoping no one would ever recognise me again!"

The following day ML 407 was taken on charge by the Squadron and selected and test-flown by F/O Johnnie Houlton, a 21-year-old from Christchurch, New Zealand. The aircraft was to become his regular "mount" for the next few months and was taken under the aegis of an inseparable trio of friends, Flight Mechanics Ron White, fitter, Vic Strange, rigger, and Michael "Paddy" Fahy, electrician.

Air Transport Auxiliary (ATA)

ATA was formed originally to provide pilots for the National Air Communications Scheme, which was the brain-child of Sir Francis Shelmerdine (Director General of Civil Aviation at the Air Ministry) and was intended to operate civil aircraft requisitioned by the Air Ministry for courier, mail, ambulance and other civil defence services. All normal means of communication were fully expected to be knocked-out by immediate catastrophic bombing following the declaration of war. In addition, to release its own pilots from non-operational flying duties, the wartime RAF might well need civilian pilots.

The task of identifying likely

Jackie Sorour in Spitfire Mk IX BS 306, AE-A, of 402 (Canadian) Squadron in 1942 *(Moggridge)*.

candidates for the first requirement fell to the British Overseas Airways Corporation (formed from a merger of British Airways and Imperial Airways in August 1939). Gerard d'Erlanger, a board member of BA and a private pilot himself, was keenly interested in the project and volunteered to make up a list of experienced pilots who were, for various reasons, ineligible for Service flying.

Meanwhile, the Deputy Director General at the Air Ministry had also approached the Civil Air Guard (a Government-sponsored flying-training organisation for men and women) about the possibility of using its members for the RAF's ferrying work. However, at that time these trainees would have been lucky to have sufficient "hours" for their "A" (Private Pilot's) Licence, so it was not an immediate resource and was at best a long term solution.

On September 3rd 1939 (the day war was declared) the Air Ministry gave permission to start limited recruiting of a civil reserve of pilots. Within a week serious discussions were also begun at the Air Ministry about the loan of civilian pilots to RAF Ferry Pools.

Luckily the anticipated bombing never materialised during the "Phoney War" period and d'Erlanger's reserve of pilots remained largely unemployed. Its resources were therefore available to help the RAF. After a preliminary check-flight by a BOAC instructor, the pilots (now properly known as Air Transport Auxiliary) went to Central Flying School, Upavon, for a brief introduction to military aircraft, as eventually they would be expected to fly all types.

In February 1940 ATA headquarters was founded at White Waltham Aerodrome, near Maidenhead. Within the first year of its existence responsibility for the operational side of ATA passed first from the Air Ministry to 41 Group Maintenance Command (RAF) and then to the newly created Ministry of Aircraft Production, under Lord Beaverbrook. Central Ferry Control itself remained at 41 Group HQ, but became an ATA preserve. BOAC retained responsibility for administration, particularly personnel and pay.

At first ATA and the RAF shared ferrying duties, but eventually, as the acute shortage of operational pilots continued, ATA took over all ferry-flying, including moving aircraft from the MUs to the squadrons in the field. In 1944 Commodore d'Erlanger, in command of ATA, said, "Every machine you see in the sky has been, or will be flown at some period of its life by a pilot of the ATA."

About 15% of ATA pilots were women, who by the summer of 1943 were integrated with and employed on the same terms as the men (including pay). They had been flying operational single-engined aircraft (and then "twins") since the second half of 1941 and by autumn 1943 were moving on to four-engined bombers.

ATA had six Classes of aircraft.
I. Training and simpler operational singles
II. All other single-engined types
III. Light twin-engined types
IV. All other twins
V. All four-engined aeroplanes
VI. Flying Boats

Eventually ATA ran its own training school and a joint conversion scheme with the RAF for Classes V and VI.

During the war more than 308,000 ferry-trips were made, by a total of 1,152 male and 166 female pilots and 197 other aircrew, for the loss of 153 personnel. Flights included cross-channel deliveries when the Allies were established on the Continent.

ATA was disbanded on November 30th 1945, when the RAF felt it could once more take care of its own ferrying requirements. However ATA remains as a striking example of how the enthusiasm, imagination and dedication of one man, Gerard D'Erlanger, and his small "amateur" team could turn an idea into a mature and indispensable component of the structure of wartime air power.

485 (New Zealand) Squadron
135 Airfield, 84 Group, 2nd TAF at A.L.G. Selsey

485 Squadron pilots and ground-crew grouped around S/Ldr J. B. Niven's Spitfire NH 321, Funtington, July 1944 *(Strange)*.

"ML 407 was special as it was my first brand-new aircraft, straight from the factory. With 24 pilots, but only 18 aircraft on a squadron, one's personal aircraft had to be flown by other pilots as well, but there was a protocol involved and the 'owner' could usually indicate who should – or should not – fly his particular aircraft. As every pilot and car driver knows, there are noticeable differences

23

("Spitfire Strikes" Johnnie Houlton – John Murray, 1985)

between supposedly identical aircraft and vehicles, and ML 407 was in a class of its own."

Later that day (Sunday, April 30th), Houlton's ground crew painted the 485 Squadron code letters on one side of the fuselage roundel and the individual code letter on the other, and ML 407 became "OU-V" in time to fly her first operation next day. Poor weather however, caused the recall of the Squadron and the Bostons which were to be escorted to a target just across the Channel. It was not until a week later that F/Lt Keith Macdonald took OU-V over to Hesdin in the Pas de Calais, as one of the four Spitfires escorting eight more of 485 Squadron, each of which was carrying one 500-pound bomb. The target being obscured by cloud, the secondary target was bombed with moderate results. It was an army headquarters buildings, undefended by flak, and no enemy fighters were encountered throughout the operation.

Prelude to Invasion

Over the next few days ML 407 took part in more escort duties, as just one of the fighters in one of several squadrons assigned to protect formations of American medium bombers (Bostons and Marauders). Often as many as 72 bombers were engaged in these short-range daylight raids, which were primarily directed upon road and rail junctions, as part of the overall plan to sever the transportation links between Germany and the intended invasion area of Normandy.

During the second week in May, 485 Squadron switched from straightforward escort duties, to a period of intense dive-bombing activity. Normally eight Spitfires with 500-pound bombs would be escorted by four unencumbered fighters, their targets either V-1 launching pads (variously described as *Noball*, *Ski Sites* or *Constructional Works*) or road and rail key-points.

ML 407 dropped her first bomb in anger, on May 20th, on *Construction Works* at Eclimeux, where the Squadron achieved a good concentration around the "skis" (launching rails). Johnnie Houlton was the pilot.

"We were shown an aerial photograph of a short stretch of narrow-gauge rail line beside a wood, with a small building at the edge of the trees and given its pin-point map reference... The settings were all very much alike, with the rails of the target appearing to be elevated and ramped. We carried one 500-pound bomb under the belly of the aircraft and the run-in was made at around 8000 feet with the bomb carriers in echelon (the escorting Spitfires carried no bomb). As we peeled-off and dived, the momentary time-lag between each aircraft gave adequate separation in the dive."

485 Squadron had trained in the art of dive-bombing at an Armaments Practice Camp at Llanbedr, Wales, during the third week in March.

485 Sqd pilots	ops. in ML 407
W/O E.G. Atkins	1
W/O D.F. Clarke	6
F/Sgt R.M. Clarke	7
W/O A.J. Downer	14
F/Lt O.L. Hardy	2
W/O W.A. Hoskins	1
F/O J.A. Houlton	40
F/Sgt P.T. Humphrey	1
F/O T.S.F. Kearins	6
F/Lt J.N. King	2
F/Lt K.C. Lee	11
F/Lt K.J. Macdonald	10
F/O M.C. Mayston	5
F/Lt W.A. Newenham	2
S/Ldr J.B. Niven	1
P/O H.W.B. Patterson	4
F/Lt L.M. Ralph	1
F/O A. Roberts	2
W/Cdr P.J. Simpson	1
F/O A.B. Stead	19
F/O R.H. de Tourret	2
F/O F. Transom	3
F/O L.S.M. White	1

"The technique as practiced in Wales was fairly straight-forward and a good proportion of direct hits was normally achieved. The excellent elevator- and rudder-trim and stability of the Mk IX Spitfire in a steep, fast dive, enabled the pilot to fly very accurately to the point of bomb release. The usual practice was to then keep going on down to the deck and reform each section clear of the target area. Some of the targets were undefended, but others had a respectable concentration of light flak guns which gave no encouragement to the 'Spitbombers' to hang around looking at the damage. The German gunners usually held their fire until the aircraft were committed to the dive, probably not wishing to draw attention to their target area, in case we were just passing by.

"The 500-pound bomb was carried on a removable rack beneath the aircraft and released by a battery-operated solenoid when a button on the control stick was pushed. While on the run-up to the target the bomb was 'armed' by closing a switch on the instrument panel. During May we were told that if the bomb did not release and could not be shaken loose, the pilot should point his aircraft out to sea and bale-out, but no technical reason was given for such a drastic solution to what seemed like a hypothetical problem. However, on the next bombing trip my own bomb failed to drop away and after I had wrenched the aircraft around in a variety of violent efforts to dislodge it, I was certain that the electrical release had failed. With the arming switch returned to 'safe' therefore, I went in to land at Selsey.

Instead of the usual three-point landing, which can cause a jolt, I 'wheeled' the aircraft gently onto the ground with the tail-wheel high and then felt a solid thud while the tail kicked up a little higher. The bomb had dropped off, as the wheels touched the ground, then bounced and dented the belly of the aircraft, right back near the tail.

"My faithful ground-crew were in a state of shock, but in my ignorance I was too furious to be frightened, as I could not understand it at all. Johnnie Niven (the Commanding Officer) tore a very large strip off me and when Johnnie Walker – the Airfield Commander – came into the bar that night he called me some choice names too. Then he brought me a beer."

("Spitfire Strikes")

May 21st brought another type of operation, part of a massive effort orchestrated by the Allied tactical units that day. Operating at low-level over northern France, it involved some 500 Spitfires, Thunderbolts and Typhoons. 485's squadron-strength *Sweep* across the area between the Seine and Somme rivers resulted in the destruction of a locomotive and a "tracked vehicle". "B" Flight Commander F/Lt K. C. Lee (flying ML 407) and F/O Al Stead were responsible for the tank near Beauvais.

Next day a similar *Ranger* produced results for a Section of four Spitfires from 485 Squadron. This time Johnnie Houlton, as Section Leader, was flying ML 407.

FM(A) Vic Strange and FM(E) Ron White – ML 407's Ground-crew

F/O Johnnie Houlton with his ground-crew, Ron 'Knocker' White (fitter), Reg Gower (armourer), Vic Strange (rigger), 'Ginger' Gibson (radio), and Michael 'Paddy' Fahy (electrician), Selsey, June 12th, 1944. The aircraft is his Spitfire ML 407, OU-V *(Houlton)*.

When he was "called-up", Welsh-born Vic Strange chose the RAF because he already had two brothers in the Navy and two in the Army. His semi-skilled experience on Handley Page Hampdens "in civvy street" (until the works was bombed) marked him out for training as an airframe "fitter". He trained at Squires Gate, Blackpool and was posted first to 253 (Hyderabad State) Squadron at Hibbaldstow, which was operating Hurricanes at night, working with Turbinlite Havocs. After three months he was posted south to Kenley and joined 485 (New Zealand) Squadron, as a Flight Mechanic, Airframes, or FM(A).

Already in residence was Ron White, a steady and unflappable "engine-fitter" from Faversham. He had trained at Halton and West Freugh as a Flight Mechanic, Engines, or FM(E) and joined the Squadron earlier at Redhill. These two young men became pals and together with Paddy Fahy, an Irish electrician with a fine voice and a banjo, they became an inseparable trio. Most of the time they lived under canvas, sharing the tent with another threesome, Sammy Waldren, Pete Bradley and Alfie Blagden.

The working day was long, starting at dawn (before dawn in winter, when the aircraft engines needed to be thoroughly warmed). Paddy would check the electrics and Ron start with a visual once-over of the Spitfire's Merlin engine. He would then climb into the cockpit, prime the engine and fire it up. As it warmed-up he checked all temperatures and pressures, radiator flaps and magnetos. When the oil and coolant temperatures were right, the two-speed two-stage supercharger was checked for correct functioning and at the same boost setting (zero psi), the constant speed propeller was exercised and the charging of the accumulators by the generator confirmed. Having checked the magnetos again and with three "lucky" airmen on the tail, he would then open the throttle "up to the gate" (2,800 – 2,900rpm). For the lads on the tail the propeller blast could be an ordeal and bitterly cold in winter.

Meanwhile, Vic would be doing his rigger's checks on the airframe, making sure that the fabric (both metal and linen) was in good condition, all control surfaces giving full and free deflection (and free from foreign bodies such as dirt, leaves or ice depending upon the season), and trimmer-tabs undamaged. The undercarriage was scrutinised for obstructions which might cause retraction problems, hydraulics for correct extension and pressure, tyres for wear, inflation and fit. Fully-charged carbon-dioxide and oxygen bottles had to be aboard and the cockpit canopy free and fully lockable. If everything checked out positively, the check-list could be ticked off and the "Form 700" issued declaring the aircraft ready for flight.

In contrast to the hard work, Vic still recalls their exuberance when their Spitfire returned from an operation, "the excitement when it came back and had seen action, which we knew because of the busting of the fabric patches over the leading edge. We used to do cartwheels with excitement and call 'Action! Action!' We couldn't get Johnnie out of the cockpit quick enough to see if he'd bagged one."

Their 21-year-old pilot, Johnnie Houlton, was younger then either of them (Ron was 24 and Vic 25 in 1944) but was also a member of the team. They remember him as "smashing – one of the boys. We often went for a drink together when the Squadron was on 'stand-down'." He seemed very young and boyish to Vic, open and confident and very proud of Vicki, his girl-friend. For his part, Johnnie maintained that it was a privilege to be allowed to fly their Spitfire, which they worked so hard to keep 100% serviceable and he always shared equal credit with them. On June 12th a Press Photographer happened to be on hand at Selsey when he returned from shooting-down a Messerschmitt and wanted to take his picture. Johnnie would only allow it if his ground-crew were included because, he declared, he could not have been successful without their dedicated back-up.

Vic and Ron agree that they were lucky to be on a New Zealand Squadron, where morale and efficiency was high, despite a much more easy-going attitude towards "bull" and petty discipline than on many regular RAF squadrons. Officers and other-ranks were on friendly terms, pilots and ground-crews sharing a beer and confidences. "Where else would you find a Wingco leaning on the wing tip chatting and joking with you?"

Flight Lieutenant K.C. Lee

(IWM).

Ken Lee joined the RNZAF from the Civil Reserve in 1939. Once in England he was posted first to 4 (Army Co-operation) Squadron to fly the North American Mustang I, but after only a few weeks transferred to 485 Squadron. By 1944 he was "B" Flight Commander and flew ML 407 on 11 sorties. On May 21st with F/O Al Stead he destroyed a German tank near Beauvais in ML 407. "Al dived down and I followed. He strafed the tank – it could have been an armoured carrier or self-propelled gun – and I followed him into the attack. Pulling up and away I called Al and said it was time he got to hell out of it, as light flak was streaming up behind him. Al called back 'have a look behind yourself' – which I did – and we both kept on going at high speed."

From 1950 to '56 Lee was S/Ldr in Command of the Engineering Squadron at RNZAF Ohakea and left the Service to join the Cable Price Corporation, building and supplying the Fletcher Fu 24 agricultural aircraft.

Flight Lieutenant Keith Macdonald DFC

Keith Macdonald was a flying instructor for two years early in the war, flying Fairey Gordons for some of the time. After two short tours in the Pacific (Guadalcanal) area, he transferred to RAF Fighter Command, arriving in the UK in September 1943 aboard SS *Colombia Star*. He joined 485 (NZ) Squadron in February 1944 as a supernumerary Flight Lieutenant and flew as "number three" to Johnnie Houlton on D-Day, sharing the destruction of the second Ju 88 shot down that day. In all, he flew ML 407 on ten sorties. Subsequently he served as a Flight Commander on 222 (Natal) Squadron and was awarded the DFC before commanding 485 Squadron from February to June 1945.

In a total of 2,369 hours and 45 minutes he flew 21 types including de Havilland DH.82 Tiger Moth, Bell P-39 Airacobra, Spitfire, Curtiss P-40 Kittyhawk and Warhawk, Hawker Hurricane, Typhoon and Tempest and Focke Wulf Fw 190. He survived five forced landings, two mid-air collisions, one ditching and baled-out once.

(Macdonald).

* The Spitfire he was flying on that occasion (MK 732, OU-U) is now flying again with the Dutch Spitfire Flight.

"The lack of enemy reaction to the escorted bombing raids and dive-bombing sorties was becoming monotonous and after some badgering, Group HQ finally approved my request to fly a *Ranger* exercise. This was a refinement of the *Rhubarb* where the four aircraft now crossed into occupied territory at, or above, 8,000 feet (to avoid the intensive light flak in coastal areas) then dived to ground-level and followed a pre-arranged track, before turning for home and climbing again before crossing the enemy coast. Group Operations insisted that there should be adequate cloud above the area being penetrated, to provide cover in the event of being jumped by German fighters. I planned a route into northern Holland which would take us past a group of airfields from which German night-fighters were operating. We knew that air-tests were often flown in the afternoon by the Germans, ready for night operations, and it was hoped to intercept some of the air-testing aircraft. Otherwise there were always military targets or transport to be attacked.

"We topped-up with fuel at Manston and flew out over the North Sea and over the Frisian Islands, to find that the cloud cover ended at the Dutch coast, so I turned the Section to fly in line abreast parallel with the coast, about 10 miles inland at 8,000 feet. Two large, stationary, vehicles could be seen under the poplar trees lining a long, straight road. I took the Section down to ground-level, 10 miles further on, then turned and flew back to one side of the road, putting the Section into long line astern. Pulling up at the right point I sighted two Tiger tanks parked close together, each with a wheeled fuel-tanker behind and fired a long burst into the four vehicles before pulling up over the poplars. The scene erupted in a dense, burgeoning cloud of black smoke laced with orange flame and each of the other three pilots also put a decent burst into the targets. Normally the Spitfire Mk IX armament of 20 mm guns and 0.5-inch machine guns was capable of only minor damage to the running gear of a heavy tank and would not penetrate the tank itself, but these two would have been well and truly gutted by the burning fuel.

"Pat Patterson was flying as my sub-Section Leader with Doug Clarke as his 'number two', and after the attack, for reasons which Pat never satisfactorily explained, he elected to break away in the opposite direction from where I was heading to reform the Section."

The Section turned for home, finding time to attack a troop bus, blowing the roof away and shoot up a party of cycling troops who were unfortunate enough to cross its path. Some minutes later a light flak position opened up on Pat and Doug, so Pat turned in and took to the guns head-on. A shell exploded in the starboard half of his fixed tail-plane, opening it up like a large, ragged tin can and creating tremendous drag, or braking effect, on that side of the aircraft and causing it to slew violently.

"Doug Clarke watched in awed fascination as Pat fought the aircraft upwards in a bucking climb, like a broaching Marlin on a deep-sea rod. The German gunners

P/O "Pat" Patterson, probably photographed on June 12th 1944 *(Kearins)*.

kept shooting, but they must have been confused by the gyrations of the Spitfire and with its speed, now back to 90 mph but still gaining height. Pat was an outstanding pilot and physically very strong which, I am certain, were the reasons for his survival that day. He nursed the Spitfire up to about 6,000 feet and dragged it all the way back to Bradwell Bay.

"Pat found that below 120 mph with full left rudder he could keep it going in the right direction, but each time his stiffly-braced left leg relaxed with numbness, the aircraft stalled and plunged nose down, requiring full power and strenuous juggling to regain something near level flight. He lowered the undercarriage whilst still high enough to bale-out if necessary, then flew the aircraft down onto the runway at Bradwell Bay in a fast wheel-landing. Apart from a garbled burst of profanity I had heard nothing more over the R/T and failing to locate Pat and Doug, headed back to Manston with my 'number two'. By the time we learned Pat was down safely, the daylight was gone, so we had a pleasant 40-minute night-flight to Selsey, landing by the light of the paraffin flares. Pat was flown back to Selsey

The tail-plane of ML 400, OU-N, which P/O "Pat" Patterson flew back from Holland after being hit by light flak on May 22nd 1944 *(Roddis)*.

next day in an Auster, bringing with him a photograph of the wrecked tail-plane, which once more demonstrated the strength and durability of the graceful Spitfire."

ML 407's eventful first month with 485 Squadron was rounded off with a couple of dive-bombing sorties against *Noball* targets, at Maison Ponthieu on the 24th and Compagne-les-Hesdin on the 30th. Squadron Leader Commanding, J. R. Niven, summarised the month's activities thus.

"This month has seen the highest number of operational hours flown (525.25) by the Squadron since September 1943. During the 359 operational sorties flown not one enemy aircraft was seen and the Squadron had to be content with claiming one locomotive destroyed, one tracked vehicle destroyed, two Mk V or VI tanks damaged and one troop bus damaged."

In the broader perspective, in the period May 20th to 28th, Allied tactical strikes specifically aimed at stationary and running locomotives had damaged 500. The effects of Bomber Command's night attacks against marshalling yards and junctions, combined with American daylight raids on similar targets, had reduced rail traffic to 55% of its level in the preceding January.

The German army depended upon the railways to move reserves and supplies to the battle front, much of its infantry equipment still being horse-drawn. By the time of the invasion in Normandy, it was extremely difficult to redeploy forces with the necessary haste to counter the Allied advance. Destruction of the Seine bridges by fighter bombers in late May reduced rail traffic on French railways to 30% by D-Day, and beyond that to 10%. By mid-June the French railways had virtually ceased to operate. It was almost impossible to move mechanised units along the roads of north-west France in daylight, such was the level of low-level air attack by Allied fighters and fighter-bombers. At night the same mechanised units found roads and bridges collapsed, cratered and hazardous to negotiate. The success of this campaign of "*interdiction*" against rail- and road-movement, in the weeks leading up to the invasion, was a major factor in the winning of the subsequent battle. The German army simply could not match the build-up of men and material sustained by the invaders.

By the beginning of June about 90 fighter squadrons were packed into the south-west corner of Sussex. In several cases the landing strips were so close together that circuit patterns overlapped and had to be flown at different heights to avoid the risk of collision. Even though the Army made an effective job of camouflaging encampments and buildings, it surprised the occupants of the tented cities that the *Luftwaffe* failed to attack the build-up area.

On June 3rd orders came from HQ 2nd TAF to over-paint all aircraft with bold black and white stripes around main-planes and rear fuselage after the last sortie of the day (2nd TAF ASIO No. 19). With an estimated umbrella of more than 1,000

P/O "Pat" Patterson and his ground-crew beside MK 732, OU-U, "Baby Bea V". In the background is ML 407, OU-V. The two aircraft have black and white stripes (for ease of identification during the Normandy invasion) which were applied on June 3rd and partially removed on July 3rd 1944. "Baby-Bea V" was restored to airworthiness in 1992 by the Dutch Spitfire Flight *(Patterson)*.

aircraft of many different types above the invasion-shipping and beach-head at all times, it was essential that friend and foe should be easily identified. Begun after aircrews were "stood down" on the evening of the 3rd, the painting was hastily completed by the ground-crews, who were issued with white-wash brushes and drums of oil-bound distemper.

Since the last dive-bombing raid on June 2nd, 485 Squadron's ground-crews had worked over their aircraft even more thoroughly than usual to ensure top line serviceability for the "Big Show" which was obviously very near at hand. The pilots were able to relax for two or three days, until all personnel were confined to camp, to ensure complete security, on June 5th. At 10.30 pm that night the pilots of 485 Squadron were called to the briefing tent and as they listened, the revelations of the briefing officer were interrupted by the roar of glider tugs and transport aircraft, using the aerial corridor established between England and the invasion beaches. Selsey Bill itself, 110 miles from Normandy, was the marker from which aircraft set course.

135 Airfield, 84 Group, 2nd TAF

Designated 135 Airfield and occupied by 222 (Natal), 349 (Belgian) and 485 (New Zealand) Squadrons, Selsey was a grass strip built on the property of Mr Norman Holden. The house was built on the site of an ancient Priory, and the airfield was basically a development of his own pre-war private landing strip. Well used to entertaining RAF pilots in peacetime, his estate had now been occupied by the tented encampment of hundreds of air- and ground-crew. The pilots' tents were pitched in the tennis courts, Officers' and Sergeants' Messes in a couple of estate houses only a short walk from the crew-room tent and adjacent to the aircraft dispersal area. 485 Squadron was no stranger to the Chichester area, having operated from two airfields in the "Tangmere Sector" (Westhampnett and Merston) during the first half of 1943.

These three squadrons were the initial units of 135 Wing of 84 Group, which comprised 10 Wings in all. 83 Group and 84 Group were intended to be the spearhead of 2nd Tactical Air Force and were equipped with Spitfires, Typhoons and Mustangs. 85 Group

485 (NZ) Spitfire Squadron, Funtington, August, 1944. Standing: Orderly Cpl Len Jordan, F/Sgt Doug Clarke, F/O "Chalky" White, F/O Jack Yeatman, F/O Al Stead (KIA), F/Sgt Pat Patterson, F/Lt Lyn Black (KOAS), S/Ldr Johnnie Niven (CO), F/Lt Owen Hardy, F/Sgt Frank Transom, W/O Terry Kearins, F/O Des O'Halloran, F/O "Red" Roberts, F/Lt Keith Macdonald, F/Sgt "Mac" McInness (KOAS), F/Sgt Max Collett. Sitting: F/Sgt Eddie Atkins, W/O Athol Downer, F/Lt Bill Newenham, F/O Roy de Tourret, F/O Johnnie Houlton, W/Cdr Ray Harries (KIA), P/O Hutton (Sqd Adj), F/O Don Taylor (KIA), F/O Pete Robinson, F/Lt "Tiger Mac" Ralph, F/O Maurice "Red" Mayston, F/Sgt Russ Clarke *(Houlton)*.

would be a highly mobile defensive shield for the Allied armies once they had landed on the Continent, with Spitfires, Tempests and Mosquitos. There was also a light day-bomber component drawn from Bomber Command, entitled 2 Group, with Bostons, Mitchells and Mosquitos. The commanders of 83 and 84 Groups were Air Vice Marshals H. Broadhurst and L. O. Brown. Harry Broadhurst was an ex-Desert Air Force man.

2nd TAF itself was created in the summer of 1943, for the specific purpose of over-flying the Second Front, although its units remained part of their existing Fighter or Bomber Command Group system until November, when Air Marshal Arthur Coningham took command. Coningham was a New Zealander who had commanded the Western Desert Air Force, which had pioneered the techniques of close tactical support for ground forces soon to be applied in Europe. The use of the fighter-bomber as "aerial artillery" was foremost of these methods, other innovations being shared Headquarters for Air Force and Army Commanders and the use of mobile Air Command Posts (ACPs) with the forward troops, sometimes in direct radio contact with the aircraft overhead. Airstrip construction units would be backed-up by refuelling and re-arming parties, efficient repair and recovery units, and well supplied daily servicing echelons which were mobile enough to keep up with a rapidly advancing front line.

2nd TAF was intended to fight alongside the United States 9th Tactical Air Force which was organised on broadly similar lines for the benefit of the American ground forces.

The Commanding Officer of 135 Airfield was Group Captain P. R. "Johnnie" Walker who had been prominent in the Battles of France and Britain in 1940. His Second in Command (Airfield Commandant) was W/Cdr Fred Rosier, another veteran of the Battle of Britain who had also fought in the Western Desert.

A "Section" of 485 Squadron Spitfires including OU-X, OU-P and OU-M patrolling in close "finger-four" formation, 1944 *(Patterson)*.

Neptune and Overlord

135 Wing was to be among the first day-fighter wings to patrol the invasion beaches. At this stage of *Overlord* the operation was still known by the code-name *Neptune*, which was the cross-Channel phase of the Normandy landings.

"The immediate object of this Combined Allied Naval, Military and Air operation (was) to secure a bridge-head on the coast of France from which further offensive operations could be developed", recorded the 84 Group Operations Record Book.

On the morning of June 6th Johnnie Houlton was about to fire up ML 407.

"The engine failed to start up on the first attempt, and I ended up chasing the other 11 aircraft to the take-off point. To reach my position with the second Section, I swung wide round the tail-enders, then clamped on the brakes as the remains of a telephone, a wooden chair and my propeller tips sprayed up in front of me. The Flying Controller, carried away with the occasion, had planted a field telephone on a chair on the edge of the marshalling area. The Airfield Commandant leapt from his car using rude words, but was persuaded to drive me at high speed back to the dispersal area, where I climbed into a reserve aircraft (ML 176) and took off 10 minutes behind the Squadron. Altogether it was a bad start to a very big day."

It meant a swift propeller change for ML 407, a job which could easily be done within a couple of hours with the resources on hand at the airfield and luckily there was no other damage. This effectively kept the aeroplane out of the action until the afternoon, when Houlton's Flying Log Book records OU-V as his aircraft for another *Beach Patrol*.

"In mid-afternoon I led Blue Section during the third patrol of the day, the other Section pilots being Maurice Mayston, Keith Macdonald and Eddie Atkins. South of Omaha Beach, below a shallow, broken layer of cumulus, I glimpsed a Ju 88 above cloud, diving away fast to the south. Climbing at full throttle I saw the enemy aircraft enter a large isolated cloud above the main layer, and when it reappeared on the other side I was closing in rapidly. Our aircraft were equipped with the gyro gunsight which eliminated the snap calculations or guesswork required to hit a target aircraft – especially one in a reasonably straight flight-path – and it also enabled the guns to be used accurately at a far greater range than before. I was well aware, however, that most pilots were sceptical of the new instrument and preferred to use the conventional type of sight, which was still incorporated on the screen of the new sight. Normally one would open fire only at ranges below 250 yards, but I adjusted the gyro sight on to the target at 500 yards with a deflection angle of 45 degrees, positioned the aiming dot on the right-hand engine of the enemy aircraft and fired a three-second burst. The engine

1: June 6th 1944, D-Day. Johnnie Houlton closes on the first Junkers Ju 88 *(all photos IWM)*.

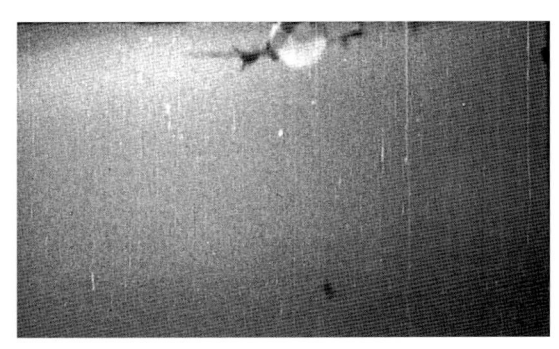

2: Macdonald's camera records the crew bailing out.

3 Houlton's guns stop the starboard engine of the second Ju 88.

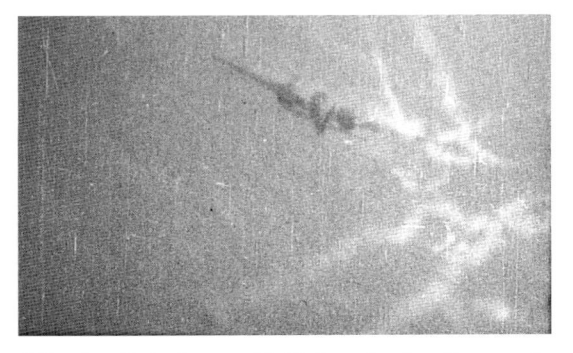

4: Mayston attacks the second Ju 88. Accurate return-fire scores 5-6 hits, damaging his oil cooler and pitot-head, but without effect.

5: Atkins' attacks the second Ju 88.

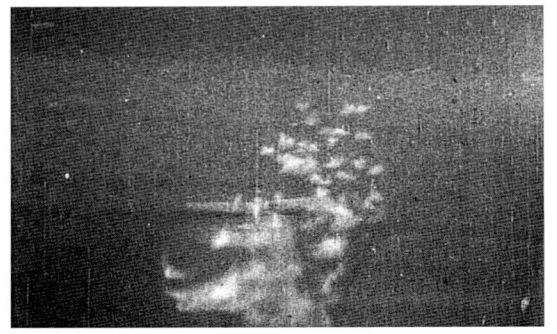

6: Atkins' cannon and machine gun fire bursting on the ground beyond the crashing Ju 88.

disintegrated, fire broke out, two crew members baled out and the aircraft dived steeply to crash on a roadway, blowing apart on impact.

"As I turned back towards the beach-head I sighted a second Ju 88 heading south and made an almost identical attack, which stopped the right-hand engine. This aircraft then went into a steep jinking dive, with the rear gunner firing at the other members of my Section who all attacked, until the Ju 88 flattened-out and crash-landed at high speed. One of its propellers broke free, to spin and bound far away across the fields and hedges like a giant Catherine wheel. As we reached the beach-head radio chatter indicated that other pilots were dealing with another German bomber, so this belated effort appeared to have been a costly exercise for the *Luftwaffe*.

"By now, two lines of ships were ranged towards the beaches, with two more lines of unloaded ships heading back. As we flew back over the in-bound lanes, the two lines of ships advancing up and down Channel to the turning point for Normandy stretched right back to the visible horizon. The Squadron's fourth patrol at dusk was uneventful. And so ended D-Day, Intelligence reports confirmed that the Army was ashore in strength, there was no doubt that the invasion had succeeded and an overwhelming mood of relief had replaced the tension of the preceding days.

"Supreme Headquarters nominated the first Ju 88 I had destroyed as the first enemy aircraft to be shot down since the invasion began, putting 485 (NZ) Spitfire Squadron at the top of the scoreboard for D-Day. Some days before the invasion I had casually suggested we should run a sweepstake for the first pilot to shoot down an enemy aircraft after the invasion began and I duly collected a few shillings from the pool. When we later had time to unwind and celebrate, my modest winnings were well short of the cost of that party."

Johnnie Houlton remembers and his Log Book entry for June 6th confirms that OU-V was the Spitfire he was flying during this action (though the 485 Squadron ORB records the aircraft as MK 950).

ML 407 flew four more *Beach Patrols* before "our second patrol late in the afternoon of June 8th came alive when 222 Squadron reported enemy aircraft flying inland above the Ouistreham Canal."

Johnnie Houlton and ML 407 were at the head of a Section (four Spitfires) which was spread out in a well-spaced line abreast formation which allowed each pilot to search the sky efficiently, and yet to cross-cover the other pilots of his Section.

"I was leading Blue Section below cloud, flying straight at the canal from the east, and called for the Section to make a steep climbing turn to the right up through the cloud layer. By sheer luck three of us emerged behind a formation of 20 Me 109s, and ahead of some pursuing Spitfires which were out of range. Frank Transom and Pat Patterson were still with me and we latched on to three of the tail-enders. The whole German gaggle – which was flying in three sections in loose line

Wing Commander P. J. Simpson DSO, DFC.

A pilot in the Battle of Britain, with 111 and 64 Squadrons, Peter Simpson was awarded the DFC on completion of his first tour when his "score" was 6 1/3 enemy aircraft. In 1941 he became a Flight Commander of 66 Squadron, between July 1942 and January 1943 the CO of 130 Squadron and from July to September of 504 Squadron (when he was also Wing Leader of 145 (FF) Airfield, Perranporth in 34 Group 2nd TAF). Transferred in March 1944 to 135 Airfield, Hornchurch, he led the Wing throughout the invasion period until July, when he embarked on a lecture tour in the USA. Although he flew ML 407 only once, he was her highest ranking pilot. Awarded the DSO, his final tally stands at 16 enemy aircraft destroyed *(IWM)*.

astern – began porpoising in and out of another cloud layer close above us. It was an unusual and frustrating sensation following these undulations and trying to line up for a short burst each time the target briefly popped out of the cloud. By my fourth attempt I was about 50 yards behind and closing fast when the Me 109 reappeared and pulled up again. This time I followed him into the cloud, firing a long burst as OU-V bounced around in his slip-stream and just as I heard Frank's unmistakable yell over the R/T 'I've got the bastard' a great blob of black smoke and debris came back at me through the murk and I half-rolled to break cloud simultaneously with the Me 109, which was trailing smoke and diving for the deck. Two other Me 109s were going down in flames – one destroyed by Frank and one by Pat – while the one I had hit started to flatten out of the dive, but crashed in a wood.

"I called Blue Section to rejoin me at the coastal end of the Canal but, shooting out from below one of the cloud layers, I found myself below and ahead of 20 Fw 190s. Calling the sighting on the R/T I broke up into the leading aircraft and the whole gaggle split outwards. Johnnie Niven – our CO – promptly arrived with his Section and a hectic melée developed. I had used all my ammunition on the Me 109, but Al Stead destroyed one Fw 190 and Johnnie Niven and Mick Esdaile damaged one each. The dog-fight drifted out over the sea into an area of very bad light and poor visibility, caused by towering black clouds against the low sun. A multitude of orange flashes and 'flaming onions' from the gloom below revealed that the Navy had, very sensibly, opened up on one and all – which rapidly broke up the party.

"After four more uneventful beach-head patrols in the next three days I suggested to the CO and Wing Operations that it would make better sense to have patrols sweeping inland in the direction of the German aerodromes, to intercept enemy aircraft before they reached the battle area. The umbrella of 1,000 fighters over the beach-head was no doubt excellent for the morale of the Army but the fact remained that some hostile aircraft were arriving over the troops and dropping bombs.

"Group Headquarters insisted that we still confine our patrols to the prescribed coastal strip, so I quietly organised my own Section to make private sweeps inland. Each member of Blue Section was to keep strict R/T silence, except in emergency. We would not be missed in the beach-head area and reckoned that if we had any success it would cancel out any 'rockets' for being absent without leave.

"Arriving over the beaches at first light on June 12th, I took Blue Section away inland, as planned. It was a beautiful clear morning and we were flying over gently rolling country, very similar to the English downs. Thirty miles south of Utah Beach I caught a glint on a lake 8,000 feet below, then picked out a tiny speck moving north. Keeping my eyes locked on to the moving object I waggled my wings and went down in a wide diving turn to identify two Me 109 fighter-bombers ahead of us and in line-astern, flying towards the beaches at zero feet.

"I hit the rear fighter-bomber with a three-second burst from 200 yards and the 109 reared up, burning fiercely and disintegrating. At about 600 feet the pilot seemed to catapult outwards and upwards, his parachute opening immediately. Then the wreckage stalled, fell and exploded in a cornfield which erupted in a sheet of flame. Unhappily for the German pilot, his parachute dropped into the heart of the fire. I then sent in my "number two", Bill Newenham, who successfully attacked the other fighter-bomber which crashed in the same area. As I expected, no awkward questions were asked as to how Blue Section happened to be so far outside the patrol area."

("Spitfire Strikes")

On June 13th the whole Squadron landed at an "R & R Strip" (Refuelling and Rearming) known as B.3, at St Croix-sur-Mer. While sitting in the cockpit of ML 407 alongside a petrol bowser, Johnnie Houlton was obliged to abandon ship with alacrity, when airmen from the refuelling and rearming party shouted to him, from a hole in the ground, to take cover. Apparently there was a sniper active from a ragged wood a few hundred yards away. After a while the all-clear whistle was blown and the aircraft were swiftly refuelled and back in the air. It was later rumoured that the sniper, who had been eliminated by a tank, was the young French widow of a German soldier who had been killed at the beach-head.

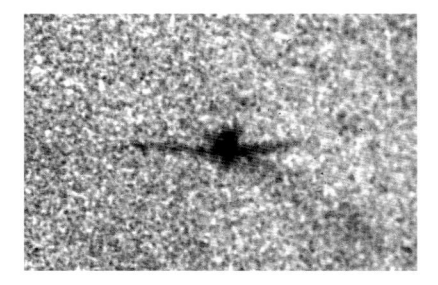

Such R & R strips were quite primitive and built by engineers, just inside the British front line, and without buildings of any sort. The airmen worked among a few earth walls and revetments with petrol bowsers and stacks of ammunition boxes, their tents dotted about the perimeter of the field. It was both uncomfortable and dangerous, but a vital part of the support necessary to a tactical air force in close support of ground forces.

Messerschmitt Bf 109 fighter-bomber under attack from ML 407, June 12th 1944 *(IWM)*.

Back at Selsey, the main pre-occupation of the ground crews from June 15th onwards was flying-bombs. The "Zombies" or "Probats" caused a good deal of consternation and regular dives into the "funk hole" as they passed overhead on the way to Portsmouth and Southampton. The airmen followed the fortunes of ADGB (Air Defence Great Britain – the home defence command replacing Fighter Command when 2nd TAF was formed) against the flying bombs with as much keenness as the efforts of their own pilots against the *Luftwaffe*.

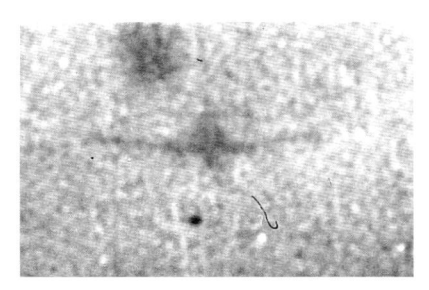

Two days later, as ML 407 took off from Selsey for another *Beach Patrol*, the starboard tyre burst at the moment of take-off. Nevertheless Johnnie Houlton completed the sortie but elected to land at Ford aerodrome, fearing that the interlaced steel rods which reinforced the grass strip at Selsey might make matters worse.

Messerschmitt Bf 109 fighter-bomber under attack by Bill Newenham, June 12th 1944 *(IWM)*.

F/O Frank Transom and to his left LAC G. Wilson, Cpl Frank Hempstead, and LAC Eddie Platten (kneeling), probably on June 12th 1944. In Wilson's belt is a cocking tool for the .5-inch Browning machine gun *(Houlton)*.

S/Ldr Johnnie Niven DFC and bar & F/Lt Bill Newenham *(Kearins)*.

"By touching-down on the left wheel with the left wing well down into the cross-wind from the same side, OU-V turned off to the right only slightly, after the weight settled onto the damaged wheel and the tail came down."

Not only did this demonstrate the docility and sensitivity of the Spitfire, but a fair degree of airmanship on his part.

The great storm of June 19th to 22nd caused enormous losses of equipment and shipping and brought the landing of stores, equipment and ammunition to a full stop at the Normandy bridge-head for four days. Shortly afterwards Johnnie Houlton and his aircraft were once more in a tricky position.

"As a brief spell of similar weather blew up we spent the night on an emergency landing strip on the beach-head, to do a special patrol at first light the following morning. Having spent a very rough night on straw in the back of army trucks, after a meal of bully beef and hard biscuits, our briefing was to return to Selsey on completion of the morning patrol. Weather conditions deteriorated into a storm after take-off, with towering thunderheads, whirling cloud layers and heavy rain packing into the Channel and over Normandy. My Section became split up in the gloom and at the end of the patrol time I let down into the cloud towards England, calling for a "homing" from Tangmere Control, as I had no real idea of my position. The radio remained silent and I eventually broke cloud below 100 feet in torrential rain above steep seas, the crests of which were being blown into clouds of

41

spray by the driving force of the gale. Forward visibility was down to about 200 yards as OU-V slipped along at reduced speed and I was well soaked in perspiration when white cliffs reared up ahead. Turning hard right I followed the shore of the Isle of Wight, then across to the mainland and into base.

"It transpired that all aircraft had been recalled to land again in Normandy because of the weather in the Channel, but my radio receiver was 'out'. The transmitter was working however, and Vicki* was on duty that morning and had plotted my homing call in her capacity as DF (Direction Finding) Teller. The homing course had been called to me by the Controller and there had been a tense 20 minutes in the Operations Room before OU-V had been checked on to the ground."

It was on June 29th that Houlton once more fired the guns of ML 407. After a two-day binge enjoyed by pilots and ground-crews together, doing the rounds of the pubs of Chichester to celebrate the successful establishment of the Allies in Europe, Johnnie Houlton was "not very well" as he trudged out to the dispersal area through dew-laden grass at 7.30 am. Indeed, it was with grave reservations that his trusted ground-crew finally acceded to his order to get him onto the wing and into the cockpit of their precious Spitfire, OU-V. But once in the seated position, he was able to convince them that he was capable of looking after their aircraft in the manner to which she was accustomed, and proved able to take-off and finish the patrol without mishap.

"After completing the dawn patrol we landed on an emergency strip on the beach-head to refuel, then carried-out a second patrol before returning to Selsey. It was a morning with jumbled cloud formation, towering build-ups and the sun mostly obscured, with vast, black caverns between the pillars of cloud. I set off after

* Later to become Mrs Johnnie Houlton.

"Pat" Patterson's Spitfire MK 732, OU-U, "Baby Bea V" being run-up at Selsey in June 1944 (Patterson).

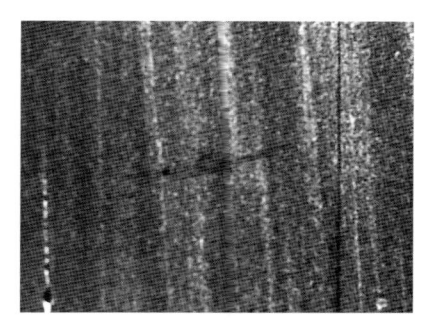

Messerschmitt Bf 109 under attack from ML 407 June 29th 1944 *(IWM)*.

("Memoirs Of The War" LAC Peter Bradley, Fitter 485 Squadron (MS)

a remote object at 8,000 feet, which I lost sight of after a couple of minutes, but in the gloom my Section also lost contact with me. So I spent some time banking, climbing and twisting between the huge masses of cumulus and through the caverns and canyons, which is an exciting way of pretending one is riding a great bird, alone in the upper air.

"As I emerged from behind a towering cloud, a lone Me 109 flew out into a patch of sunlight half a mile away and the pilot continued straight ahead as I turned in behind him. As I fired he went into the oddest evasion routine I ever encountered, slipping rapidly down and then slicing up, then down the other way and up, like slipping from side to side within a giant 'U-tube'. I followed him through the first of these gyrations, which had a shocking effect on my already uneasy stomach, so I held the line of sight steady at the top of one side of the 'U' he was creating, then fired as he came up into my sights on the return swing. There was a decent splatter of strikes on the wing, and the 109 pilot whipped round fast, to disappear into a handy cloud."

On June 30th the Squadrons of 135 Airfield moved from ALG Selsey to ALG Coolham near Billingshurst. While at Coolham, on July 3rd, the ground-crews spent an uncomfortable day scraping the black-and-white stripes off the top of the main-planes and fuselages of the Spitfires. According to Pete Bradley it was "raining like hell and then some, the mud right up to your bum, chum."

"The pilots were making regular landings on make-shift airfields in Normandy now, on runways constructed of PSP (Pierced Steel Planking) tracking so the accent was on tyre-checks when they returned, to inspect for damage. They brought back with them bottles of Vichy Water and Calvados," remembers Continuity Sergeant Joe Roddis.

"Mobility exercises came thick and fast in preparation for when our turn came to go to Normandy. At very short notice we'd pack-up everything into the fleet of vehicles we now operated, instead of having to rely on a separate MT (Motor Transport) Section. All the ground-crew were drivers of the Squadron vehicles – 3-ton Chevvies (Chevrolets), low-loaders, Commer vans, de-icer units, wireless trucks and Jeeps – and I drove the CO's Fordson V-8 shooting-brake. We made quite a convoy when on the move.

"We did a three-day mobility exercise from Selsey to Coolham and left Coolham for Funtington at the beginning of July. When I refer to 'we' I mean the whole of 135 Wing, comprising 485 (NZ), 222 and 349 (Belgian) Squadrons."

"Back at the end of 1943, 2nd TAF had brought in a few changes to personnel deployment, in anticipation of this mobile life-style. All ground-crew, with the exception of three men (the Adjutant F/O Hutton, Orderly Room NCO Cpl Len Jordan and Continuity Sgt Joe Roddis) became known as 6485 Servicing Echelon.

This applied across the board and 349 Squadron's became 6349 SE and 222 Squadron's became 6222 SE. It was just a name-change really, everyone stayed put, but the actual Squadron strength was now aircrew plus three ground staff. All to do with squadron mobility and it meant that a squadron could now move around the Group, if necessary, without all the ground-crew in the move. Wherever it went there'd be a fully experienced ground-crew to meet it.

"We liked Funtington, our tents were pitched amongst the trees at dispersal with the aircraft close-by and the weather was great. Very busy here, dawn to dusk and we always seemed to be changing overload fuel tanks. We called them droptanks and they came in various shapes and sizes. Plywood and fabric 'slipper' tanks, 30- and 45-gallon size or 50-gallon cigar-shaped metal ones. We'd been using drop-tanks for a long time now but not with the same intensity as we were doing here."

("My Time with the New Zealand Spitfire Squadron No. 485" Joe Roddis, Continuity Sgt (MS)

The move from Selsey had brought with it a reversion to *Ramrod* (bomber escort) operations, after a month almost entirely committed to *Neptune*. The Spitfires of 485 Squadron had flown more than 1,200 hours in support of the invasion of Normandy, ML 407 contributing 66 hours 45 minutes. Nine enemy aircraft were claimed destroyed and three damaged for no losses. Johnnie Houlton contributed $3^{1}/_{4}$ destroyed and one damaged. The *Luftwaffe* had only managed to put in sporadic appearances, being heavily committed on the Eastern Front and in defence of the Reich itself, in particular the synthetic fuel industry which was now the main objective of Operation *Pointblank* (the strategic bombing campaign

Pilots and ground-staff pushing S/Ldr Johnny Niven's Spitfire, NH 321, into position for a press photographer at Funtington on August 4th 1944. On the left is the CO's Fordson shooting-brake and on the right ML 354, OU-P *(Patterson)*.

against German industry). Nevertheless, in the two weeks following D-Day *Luftflotte 3* lost nearly 75% of the aircraft it had possessed on June 5th. Most of the *Luftwaffe's* ground-attack aircraft were on the Russian Front, so fighters flew the bulk of strikes against the Normandy landings. Hampered with bombs, they were easy targets for the swarms of Allied fighters. As a result of the pre-invasion bombing they were based at ill-equipped landing strips often lacking basic communications links and servicing facilities. Replacement pilots and aircraft rushed in from Germany could not keep pace with the losses.

"It was about now that the V-1 'Doodlebug' started to make its presence felt," says Joe Roddis. "There seemed to be a constant stream passing daily over our airfield. We'd watched the odd Typhoon or Tempest, and even a Spitfire, trying to catch them and tip them up to make them dive into the ground, but they were a bit too fast for the aircraft in straight-and level-flight. They became so commonplace, after a while, that if the engine of the V-1, Buzz Bomb, Doodlebug or whatever you chose to call it, kept going, we didn't even bother to look up. When the engine stopped it meant it was about to drop on you and explode and we didn't wait to find out where it would land.

"A few of the lads had elected to pitch their tent on the opposite side of the dispersal from us, in front of a huge collection of drop-tanks. The lads – Harry

Armourer Pat Beale cleaning the barrel of a 20 mm cannon. Note the external electrical power-supply cable for the starter-motor of the Spitfire *(Patterson)*.

F/Lt Lyn Black, F/O "Chalky" White, W/O Athol Downer, W/O Mick Esdaile (on the nose), P/O Pete Robinson, S/Ldr Johnny Niven, P/O "Pat" Patterson and W/O Doug Clarke (on the wing), F/Lt "Tiger Mac" Ralph, F/O Roy de Tourret and F/O Maurice "Red" Mayston with the CO's Spitfire NH 321 at Funtington, August 4th 1944.
(Patterson).

("My Time with the New Zealand Spitfire Squadron No. 485")

Mihalop, Tom Prickett, Archie Jackson, 'Ginger' Archer and Tony Moore – were all quietly enjoying the usual 'cuppa' during a break when a V-1 appeared and the engine stopped! It dived towards the pile of drop-tanks and landed with an ear-splitting crash, throwing earth, drop-tanks and debris everywhere. Everyone watching set off at a gallop towards the lone tent, expecting to find the occupants crushed and were met half-way by them, galloping towards us, completely unscathed! The drop-tanks had absorbed the full blast and protected them from injury or possible death!"

Actually, the RAF Regiment anti-aircraft gunners had begun firing upon the V-1 as it approached, rather than waiting until it had passed overhead. That their marksmanship was not rewarded with the loss of many lives and aircraft was nothing short of miraculous. Another was seen to explode in the air when fired at by an aircraft. In retaliation the Squadron performed several *Ramrod* duties, escorting Lancasters and Halifaxes to *Noball* sites.

"There were rarely any serious attacks by the Luftwaffe against these RAF bomber streams, and we repeatedly saw our bombers carry out their extremely

("Spitfire Strikes")

accurate attacks on V-1 sites, under what the bomber crews no doubt felt were ideal conditions. First of all they were flying in daylight, and secondly they had ample fighter protection to prevent distractions. If a crew was not satisfied with the run-in, they could turn back and regain the bomber stream for another run."

In the third week of July Johnnie Houlton was awarded the DFC (Distinguished Flying Cross) and then disappeared for several weeks on a morale-boosting lecture tour of Gyro Gunsight factories. ML 407 continued to fly regular *Ramrods* where targets included railway marshalling yards, POL (Petroleum, Oil and Lubricant) dumps, and road- and rail-junctions. Several pilots flew her, but W/O Athol Downer most often. Such was the continued effectiveness of these operations by 2nd TAF that on July 15th Rommel (Commander of the German forces on the Channel) warned Field Marshal von Kluge, the new C-in-C of the Western Front:

"Due to the disruption of the railway and the attacks carried out on major and minor roads up to 150 kilometers behind the front, only the most essential supplies can be delivered to the troops."

The early part of August was taken up by a routine of *Ramrods* in northern France, enlivened by attacks on MET (motorised enemy transport) on the return trips. In this way the Squadron accounted for a number of vehicles, and later in the month also attacked trains.

On the 8th the Squadron moved again, this time back to Selsey for a week, but on August 19th the heavy baggage was moved to the "Concentration Area" to await enshipment and later the same day the pilots, aircraft and "Air Lift Party" (essential administration staff and ground-crews) moved to RAF Tangmere to await a flight to France. After weeks under canvas the luxury of permanent beds and baths at an established RAF Station was much appreciated.

Falaise Pocket

Just before the move to Tangmere, the Squadron had escorted Marauders on "shows" in the Falaise area, and afterwards several *Armed Recces* were made at the climax of this momentous battle. Elements of the German 7th Army and 5th Armoured Army (Panzer) were fighting desperately to avoid encirclement by Canadian First Army from the North and US First Army from the South, British 2nd Army from the West and US Third Army in the East. The only route of escape was through a corridor some 25 miles long by 15 miles wide, still open at the eastern end. Between August 4th and August 20th when the pocket was sealed, the Allied ground forces and aircraft of 2nd TAF and US 9th TAF inflicted enormous losses of men and equipment upon the retreating Germans.

By the end of the battle the German Army had lost an estimated 10,000 dead and 50,000 taken prisoner. Vehicle losses amounted to some 631 tanks and self-

W/O Athol Downer in 1944. After basic flying training in New Zealand, Athol Downer arrived in the UK in January 1943. Advanced and operational training were at 7 AFU Peterborough and 53 OTU Kirton-in-Lindsay and he joined 485 Squadron at Drem in the winter of 1943-44. He flew 19 sorties (five non-operational) in ML 407 in 1944 *(Downer)*.

Flying Officer Johnnie Houlton DFC

F/O Johnnie Houlton with Spitfire ML 407, OU-V, shortly after shooting down a Messerschmitt Bf 109 June 12th 1944 *(Houlton)*.

John Arthur Houlton was born in Christchurch, New Zealand, and applied to join the RNZAF in April 1941 at the age of 18.

Trained in New Zealand under the Empire Air Training Scheme, he flew the de Havilland DH.82 Tiger Moth and North American Harvard II at EFTS, Harewood and SFTS, Woodbourne, where he won his "Wings". He arrived in England in February 1942, for operational training at 17 AFU, Watton, on Miles Masters and 55 OTU, Usworth, on the Hawker Hurricane I. In June he was posted, as a Sergeant Pilot, to 485 (NZ) Squadron to fly the Spitfire Mk V at Kenley and Kingscliffe. After a month however, Houlton volunteered for service in Malta, and subsequently flew a Spitfire to the island from the aircraft-carrier *HMS Furious*, during Operation *Pedestal*. In Malta he flew with 185 Squadron at Halfar and was credited with one Junkers Ju 52 destroyed, one probable and one damaged on 28th November.*

Back in England, he was initially posted to 602 Squadron at Westhampnett in February 1943 and continued to fly the Spitfire Mk Vb (mainly on *Ramrod* bomber escorts) but shortly returned to 485 Squadron. From another Tangmere Sector airfield, Merston, the Squadron moved to Biggin Hill on July 1st, where it was re-equipped with the Spitfire Mk IX.

In the following weeks 485 was the Sector's top-scoring squadron, Johnnie Houlton claiming one Focke Wulf Fw 190 destroyed on August 27th, two Messerschmitt Bf 109s damaged and a shared Fw 190 destroyed on September 16th. In August 1943 he was commissioned. After a spell in the Hornchurch Wing and a rest period at Drem, 485 Squadron returned to Tangmere Sector in March 1944 as a component of 135 Airfield, 2nd TAF. On D-Day Johnnie Houlton was the first Allied pilot to shoot down an enemy aircraft on the Second Front, when he accounted for a Junkers Ju 88 himself and shared another with his Section. Two days later he destroyed a Messerschmitt Bf 109 and on the 12th another. On June 29th he claimed a Bf 109 damaged.

Shortly after moving from Selsey to Carpiquet in Normandy, Houlton stood down from operations for a "rest" course at Fighter Leader School and Central Gunnery School but in Spring 1945 he returned to 135 Wing at B.77 Gilze Rijen to join 274 Squadron. On May 3rd flying a Hawker Tempest V Houlton destroyed a Dornier Do 217 which meant he had destroyed both the first and the last enemy aircraft shot down by 135 Wing. In addition to his official score of 6³/₄ aerial victories, one probable and four damaged, Johnnie Houlton destroyed two Tiger tanks, numerous MET and six aircraft in ground attacks. In August 1945 he was promoted to Squadron Leader.

Back home in New Zealand in 1946, Johnnie Houlton worked on agricultural and bush contracting until 1950 and had a spell with Straits Air Freights Express, before joining 41 (Transport) Squadron, RNZAF, for three years. From 1955 to '65 he flew Air Charter, non-scheduled Air Services and in Agricultural Aviation. In 1965 he was appointed Safety Director and Secretary of the Agricultural Pilots Association of New Zealand where he remained until 1973, meanwhile providing consultant services for various companies and organisations. In 1976 he was placed in charge of RNZN Field Station Claris, Great Barrier Island, from which he retired in 1983.

Johnnie Houlton's wartime flying experiences are graphically retold in his book *"Spitfire Strikes"* (John Murray 1985).

* The author's research in the *Luftwaffe's* surviving records suggests that all three of the Ju 52s attacked by Houlton that day may have been destroyed.

Miles Master IIs from 17 AFU (Advanced Flying Unit) Watton, in transit to Calverley in July 1944 *(Collett)*.

Originally inscribed by Terry Kearins "Johnnie flies over the ocean", August 27th 1944. ML 407, with 50-gallon torpedo-shaped overload fuel tank, is escorting Halifax and Lancaster bombers to Homberg. It was 135 Wing's first trip to "Happy Valley" (the Ruhr) and the bombers' first daylight raid. Note the beam-approach aerial-blister under belly *(Kearins)*.

ML 407, OU-V, on "B" Flight's dispersal area at Merville, September 1944 *(Collett)*.

485 Squadron Spitfires in "line astern" formation photographed through the gun-sight of F/Sgt Max Collett's aircraft. They are carrying 50-gallon "torpedo" over-load fuel tanks slung beneath the centre-section *(Collett)*.

propelled guns, 512 light armoured vehicles, 8,389 trucks, motorcycles and cars and 581 artillery pieces. Typhoons, Spitfires and Mustangs of 2nd TAF flew 9,896 sorties in the 14 days which marked the height of the battle and Lightnings and Thunderbolts of the US 9th Tactical Air Force flew 2,891. An analysis of enemy casualties in vehicles and equipment during the retreat from Normandy to the Seine, issued in October 1944, by the Operational Research Section of 21st Army HQ, concluded:

"It is considered that the evidence points to interdiction as being the primary task to be performed against a rapidly retreating enemy so that his retreat can be stopped, and that the infliction of casualties should in the first instance be of importance only in so far as it contributes towards interdiction. Once the interdiction has been established congestion must result and casualties can be inflicted at a very high rate by any weapon that can be brought to bear."

This is borne out by the subsequent operational career of ML407. As the German army pulled-back steadily northwards, the Spitfires of 2nd TAF would become ever more involved in the disruption of road and rail traffic as a primary means of supporting the Allied ground forces.

The Continent

At last on August 26th the advance party of 485 Squadron personnel left by Dakota in perfect flying weather "much to their delight and relief" for their new home, B.17, at Caen/Carpiquet airfield. Their journey was in contrast to that of the road party who spent 30 stormy hours at sea, having left four days earlier. Pilots and aircraft, delayed by more bad weather, did not make it until August 31st. "They were just in time to go down with the rest of the airfield in the current malady of acute dysentery," the Operations Record Book observed wryly.

Carpiquet had been the municipal airport of Caen, and its condition matched the devastation of the city inflicted by bombing and shellfire.

"That afternoon we flew on an armed reconnaissance (using long-range tanks) all the way up to Abbeville, and I found a convoy of enemy transport which we duly strafed and destroyed. The trucks were armed with the usual anti-aircraft guns and as I made my second attack amongst the flak everything changed... I momentarily froze as the red and green balls curved up at me and had an insane urge to wrench open the canopy and jump out."

("Spitfire Strikes")

Johnnie Houlton recognised his symptoms, known as "The Twitch", which indicated an over-dose of operational flying. As far back as April his Squadron Leader, Johnnie Niven and Airfield Commander, Johnnie Walker, had suggested it was time for a rest. But a deal had been struck to allow Houlton his crack at the Second Front, providing he let them know as soon as "The Twitch" appeared. A

S/Ldr Johnny Niven fraternising with a local, Normandy 1944 *(Patterson)*.

F/Sgt Peter Humphrey *(Humphrey)*.

* Johnnie Houlton's Log Book records one further sortie in OU-V on dawn patrol, September 1st. During this *Armed Recce* in the Hesdin area, MET was destroyed, but his Spitfire was hit by shrapnel in a coolant radiator. If it was indeed ML 407, this would be the only "Flying Battle Damage" she sustained during the war.

battle-fatigued Section Leader could be a liability to his colleagues, so it was that ML 407's first RAF pilot volunteered to stand down.*

485 Squadron began to settle into its new rôle of air support for the ground forces, during September. The month began with a number of *Armed Recces* and *Sweeps* to the north, in the Pas de Calais and even into Holland, as far as Breda. A good deal of damage was wrought on MET, HDT (horse-drawn transport), and barges and shipping in the Schelde area.

Channel Pockets and Dutch Islands

At the beginning of the second week a move was made, in the pouring rain, from B.17 to B.35 Eu near Le Tréport which lies between Dieppe and Abbeville. This enabled the Squadron to operate in close support of II Corps of General Crerar's Canadian First Army, attacking Boulogne, Calais and Dunkirk, which remained as pockets of resistance well behind the Allied front line. This association with II Corps had begun at Falaise, and was to go on for ML 407 until the end of the war.

"Our convoy weaved its way through what was left of Caen, over the river bridge hastily constructed by the Engineers. The river was full of floating bodies,

485 Squadron Spitfire about to be armed with a 500-pound bomb, Selsey, 1944. The pilots seated on the bomb trolley are W/O Mick Esdaile, P/O Pete Robinson and F/O Don Taylor *(Collett)*.

("My Time with the New Zealand Spitfire Squadron No. 485")

humans and horses etc. Eventually we stopped and made camp at what can only be described as a ploughed field. This was Le Tréport or Eu."

The greater proportion of ML 407's sorties this month were with F/O Al Stead, who was a South Island Maori from Dunedin and a top class rugby player at fly half or stand-off half. He had been with 485 Squadron since November 1943 and like Johnnie Houlton had served in Malta in 1942.

A period of intensive dive-bombing operations began in the second week of September. These were split between attacks on German defensive positions in the Dunkirk and Calais pockets, and on shipping and transport in the Walcheren and Oosterschelde area. After a lightning advance by the British 11th Armoured Division, Antwerp had been taken on September 4th, with port facilities intact. However, when General Montgomery subsequently halted the advance of 21st Army Group and turned his attention to Operation *Market Garden* (the airborne assault on Arnhem and other key-points), the German Fifteenth Army escaped entrapment on Walcheren and took up positions on the Schelde. This effectively denied the facilities of the port of Antwerp to Allied convoys for a further seven weeks.

However, as far as 485 Squadron was concerned, the dive-bombing operations proved quite rewarding, particularly targets attacked in Flushing, Bergen-op-Zoom, Turnhout, and Knokke-Heist. Not one enemy aircraft was encountered throughout the month.

But if the aircrew were enjoying some success, the ground-crews were pretty browned-off about the way things were going. "Hell of a place for rain, this, damn

Flying Officer Al Stead DFC

Al Stead was a South Island Maori from Dunedin and a dashing mid-field rugby player. He joined the RNZAF in March 1941 and was commissioned in 1943. In 1942 he volunteered for service in Malta, but having taken off from *HMS Furious* on August 11th his long range fuel tank failed, so he elected to (successfully) land his Spitfire back on *HMS Indomitable* without benefit of arrester gear. In Malta he saw considerable action with 249 Squadron and on his return to UK, in 1943 (after a six-month rest period) he continued a distinguished career with 485 Squadron. Stead claimed several enemy aircraft, including a Messerschmitt Bf 109 on June 8th 1944 but on June 10th he was forced to shoot down a Seafire in full D-Day stripes which persistently attacked him.

He flew 19 sorties with ML 407 with notable success against MET on November 30th, recorded the 485 Sqdn ORB "Three aircraft participated in an *Armed Recce*, and attacked MET claiming 4 Flamers, 2 Smokers and 5 damaged. Quite a good show."

Al Stead was killed crash-landing on January 6th 1945 after his Spitfire was hit by debris from a train he had just attacked.

(Houlton).

stuff just falls down, bags of mud too," complained diarist Pete Bradley, "but I suppose we must be satisfied with the consolation that it makes the ground softer to sleep on. We have no straw now. Who wouldn't be an airman."

They had problems with their rations too, because the cook-house staff were giving their 24-hour ration packs and chocolate to the local people, while the servicemen bartered for eggs and tomatoes in exchange for cigarettes and soap.

The airstrip at Eu left a lot to be desired. Several aircraft becoming casualties – two bogged-down and another up on its nose, smashing its propeller. A Typhoon pilot was killed in a take-off accident.

Moving on again to B.53 Merville, near Lille, in the wake of the rapidly advancing Canadian II Corps, the airmen were roused at 4 am to begin packing and were on the road by 8 am. "We reached the next airfield around September 12th, Merville, in France, not too far from Lille and a permanent place with runways. It was getting dark when I arrived and to crown a long tiring drive the Fordson shooting-brake finally gave up the ghost. The gear-box and back axle were finished and after cruising on a few yards, we got out to find ourselves, in the gloom, half-way down the main runway! When daylight came and we returned to retrieve the vehicle we discovered that both sides of the runway we were standing on had 500-pound bombs equally-spaced for the whole of its length. The Jerries must have left in a hurry before they'd had the chance to detonate them.

"Merville was one long, unending saga of rain and mud. The tents appeared to be floating and no one had any really dry gear the whole time we were there. Rations were good, all supplied by the Army catering Corps and prepared outside the Mess tent over an oil and water-trap fire. This consisted of a large metal cooking plate over a two-foot deep trench filled with Spitfire sump oil. When water was dropped onto the oil from a 5-gallon drum at each end, it blazed fiercely. Occasionally, when some intrepid aircrew sallied forth armed with .303 rifles, we had venison for dinner. I do remember," says Joe Roddis, "old Hank, the Sergeants' Mess cook, was forever frying eggs by the hundred. On the odd occasion, when the sun did appear and a few square yards of the higher ground dried-out, out would come the clothes-lines and wet clothing. It looked like Epsom Downs!"

("My Time with the New Zealand Spitfire Squadron No. 485")

" . . . I guess the good Lord turned the tap on to cool the war off a bit, kites are getting bogged down wholesale and plenty go up on their nose but that doesn't worry us. It's when our kit starts floating that we have a 'bind'," Records Bradley. "Wizard feeling to wake up in the night to find half the tent airborne and water pouring into your bed, the comfort one gets at such times can't be imagined without the actual experience. The highlight of the evening however, comes when all the earwigs, black beetles, cockroaches and other 'bloody nuisances' that have been annoying you, run for their lives up the tent pole to keep out of the wet."

LAC Vic Strange and LAC Michael Fahy "Up against the fuselage of my plane (ML 407), Belgium, December 1944" *(Strange)*.

485 Squadron Armourers' workshop and office, Merville, September 1944. "Scotty" (wireless), Joe Roddis (engine fitter), Ricky "Monty" Norman (armourer) and Frankie Adams (wireless) *(Roddis)*.

(Memoirs Of The War)

The locals, although more pleased to see the liberators than many in Normandy had been, were by now, according to Bradley, "putting up prices and stinging the poor old 'Erk'."

After the capture of Calais, which finally surrendered to Canadian 3rd Division, II Corps, on September 30th, the attention of ground support dive-bombers was directed towards the next "pocket" north-east of Bruges centred on the port of Breskens. Most of the Squadron's 25 operations in October were concerned with the bitter and costly "Battle Of The Polders" as Canadian II Corps fought with the one remaining German division, through mud and water. 485 Squadron Operations Record Book contains reports like:

"2.10.44 – 16.45 – The Squadron Dive Bombed a target south of Antwerp, scoring 12 direct hits. After bombing the Squadron did strafing attacks from east to west. A house on East of the target burned fiercely when hit."

"19.10.44 – 07.50 – The Squadron bombed and strafed in sections of four aircraft. First section off at 07.50, Last section off at 11.05. The target was ONK2 the HQ on OOSTBURG was bombed and two MET damaged. At the end of his recce Red 1 (F/Lt White) saw 100 + troops hiding round two haystacks, he called up the other two sections and all of them expended all ammo on this target."

"29.10.44 — 15.30 — Three hits obtained on a gun position containing three heavy guns, the bombing attack being followed by a strafing attack... "

PT 938 OU-T "Thunderguts" was W/O Eddie Atkins' Spitfire. LACs Pete Bradley (fitter), Charlie Taylor (rigger), Vic Strange (rigger), Ron "Knocker" White (fitter), Paddy Fahy (electrician), and Alfie Blagdon (fitter) at Maldegem, December 1944 *(White)*.

* 135 Wing Operations Record Book.

The operation on the 2nd was a particular success and illustrates what could be achieved in a well co-ordinated bombardment.

"The grand finale was done by 485, 222 and 349 who followed immediately after three squadrons of 145 Wing. The squadrons went in in turn between 17.00 and 17.30 hours to bomb and strafe a Hun C.P. (Command Post) and strong point near Turnhout which was holding the Army. After bombing each squadron made strafing attacks, the red smoke markers fell with beautiful timing between each attack so that the next one could be made where the Army wanted it. A bouquet from the Army this morning tells us that everything went excellently."*

Such specific actions would be under the control of a Forward Command Post (FCP), located close to the Army Corps Head Quarters and each Division would have its Contact Car with an RAF pilot as controller. Control of aircraft might be handed to a Contact Car from a FCP if any particular Division got beyond effective range of direct control by the FCP.

The Squadron was obviously showing increasing proficiency in the art of dive-bombing, but having to operate in steadily deteriorating weather as the autumn advanced. On 2nd three Typhoons and one Spitfire were "pranged" landing at Merville in high cross-winds and on the 12th seven Spitfires and a "Tiffey" were damaged in "nose-overs". ML 407 was one of the casualties when, on returning

F/O Allan Roberts *(Roberts)*.

Armourers Cpl Roy Andrews and Frank Jordan re-loading a .50-inch machine gun of a Spitfire Mk IXe at Maldegem in December 1944 *(Edwards)*.

from a dive-bombing and strafing attack on enemy gun positions, F/O Allan Roberts had trouble with the undercarriage refusing to lock-down correctly for landing. The fierce cross wind was no help keeping him on the runway, and the aircraft ran off into the mud and ended up on its nose.

The repairs required only amounted to "Cat.AC" and were put down to flying battle-damage, so the job was evidently completed by the airfield's own servicing echelon, 6485 SE, or its R & I "Randi" (Repair and Inspection) unit. ML 407 was posted "Re-Cat. A" a week later, although she was already back on "ops" after only five days. Accidents at this time were claiming more aircraft than flak damage, although other hazards threatened the ground-crews of 485 Squadron.

Joe Roddis recalls, "I was working on the radiator of a Spit, under the starboard main-plane and Terry Kearins did a wheels-up landing in OU-Q. He just skimmed over the top of me – I could have poked him with a long stick – and set it down, on its belly, on the grass beside the runway."

F/O Terry Kearins' Spitfire PT 532, OU-Q, at Merville, October 12th 1944 *(Patterson)*.

485 Squadron "plumbers" (armourers) at Merville, October 1944. Back row: Lofty Hill, Jack Charlton, unknown, Jimmie Astell, Dick Norman, Eddie Platten (with fag), unknown, Cpl Roy Andrews (fitter-armourer), unknown and Pete. Middle row: Jackie MacLaren (spare-time Spitfire signwriter), Bill Stringer, unknown, Steve, Cpl Armourer Frank Hempstead, F/Sgt Ernie Bongard (NZ) i/c 485 Squadron Armoury, Reg Gower, Pat Beale and unknown. Front row: Jock Dewar, unknown, George Wilson, Jim Harris, Wally Healy and unknown *(Edwards)*

Norby King shown here with a Hurricane IIb night-fighter of 43 Squadron, at Tangmere in 1942 *(IWM)*.

"Nearly had 'our time' yesterday," declares the long-suffering Pete Bradley, "a rocket came off a Tiffey and landed about four to five yards from our tent. Lady Luck was there and the darned thing didn't explode. We have got some beds off the Jerries now, very comfortable after the bare deck and just about time too as the tent is just about afloat."

On November 1st ML 407, with 485 Squadron, flew as shipping cover for the amphibious invasion of Walcheren and Beveland (The Dutch Islands) during which Canadian II Corps suffered badly because bomber-support from England was withdrawn due to bad weather and Naval support was ineffective in the face of German shore-based gunfire. However, there was no sign of enemy aircraft, the *Luftwaffe* being by now in total disarray and based almost entirely within Germany.

The next three days the Squadron provided close support to Canadian I Corps in its push from the Mark Canal north of Breda to establish the Waal Bridgehead. The German 15th Army put up fierce resistance.

November 1944 was conspicuous for its bad weather, to the extent that in two weeks operational flying only 137½ hours were flown. 485 Squadron had been at B.65 Maldegem, near Bruges, since the 3rd, one of the closest Allied airfields to the front line and with shelling from both sides all around. But for two weeks in the middle of the month the aircraft and pilots returned to Britain for Air Firing Practice at Fairwood Common, from which they returned to a mixed bag of operations to finish the month.

By this time General Student, in overall command of the German Armies in the North-West, had pulled the 15th Army into central Holland, in the face of the renewed, rapid, Allied advance. British I Corps (Canadian First Army) had liberated the area south of the Maas, and Canadian II Corps had leap-frogged eastwards to the Nijmegen area, having completed the liberation of the Dutch Islands. Antwerp was at last open to Allied shipping and German V-1 and V-2 attacks had begun on that port.

485 Squadron resumed dive-bombing and escort work for the medium bombers of 2 Group in attacks on railway, bridge and canal targets north of the Maas in order to disrupt troop and supply movements of the German 15th Army. ML 407, with Al Stead, was one of the three aircraft which participated in a particularly noteworthy *Recce*, attacking MET and claiming four "flamers", two "smokers" and five damaged. "Quite a good show," according to the Operations Record Book. Similar sorties continued into December, although a diversion was another blow at the tenacious German garrison in the Dunkirk pocket, who despite showers of both bombs and leaflets continued to hold out.

According to her "Form 78", on November 30th ML 407 was briefly taken on charge by 420 Repair and Salvage Unit (RSU) and returned to 485 Squadron on December 11th. So far no explanation has come to light. Maurice Mayston who flew her on the 30th has no record or recollection of a problem and her next documented sortie is, in any case, on December 3rd. The sort of job which might involve an RSU would be the recovery of a crashed or otherwise unflyable aircraft, perhaps damaged in a force-landing after enemy action, an engine problem, or

NH 432, OU-D, "Waipawa Special", W/O Max Collett's aircraft with 500-pound bomb, December 1st 1944, target Dunkirk *(Norman)*.

PV 156, OU-H, being guided onto the taxi-way. Usually flown by F/O D.G.L. Taylor *(Humphrey)*.

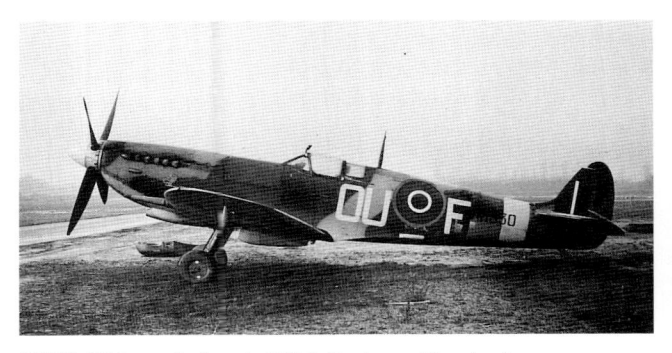

NH 530, OU-F, usually flown by W/O G. Henderson *(Humphrey)*.

PT 758, OU-J, on a very windy day in late 1944. All the photos on this page were taken at Maldegem *(Humphrey)*.

PT 857, OU-S, being refuelled. Usually flown by P/O D.F. Clarke or F/O A. Roberts *(Humphrey)*.

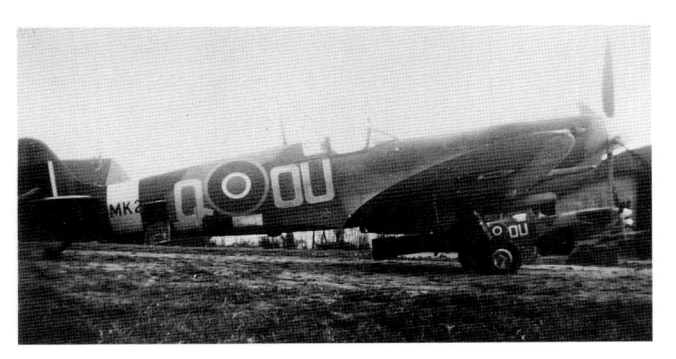

MK 288, OU-Q, with 500-pound bomb. Usually flown by F/O T.S.F. Kearins *(Humphrey)*.

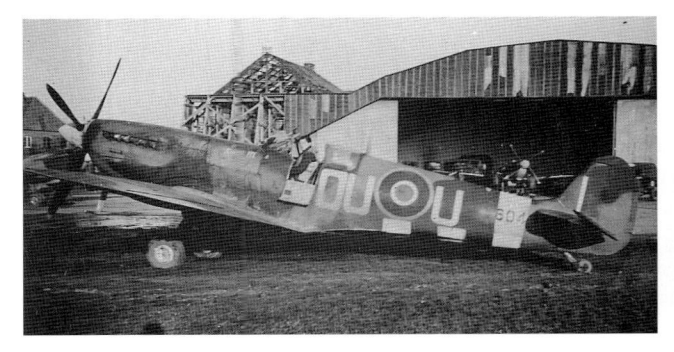

Spitfire NH 604, OU-U, "Kainui III", usually flown by W/O R.M. Clarke, at Maldegem probably November 1944 (Collett).

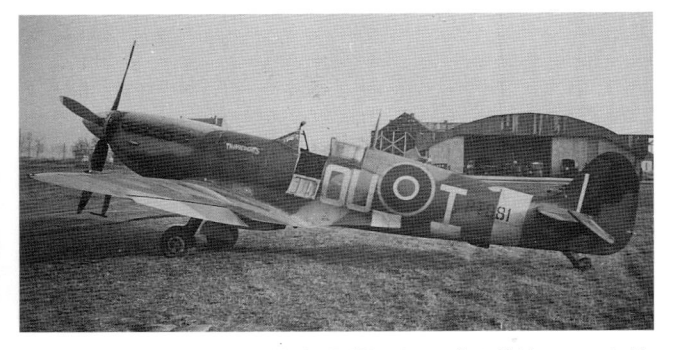

W/O Eddie Atkins' Spitfire PT 881, OU-T, "Thunderguts" at Maldegem probably November 1944 (Collet).

61

simply unable to take-off after a precautionary landing in a confined space. It is also quite probable that the paperwork lagged behind the completion of the task. It remains a mystery, but was apparently only a minor incident.

Ardennes

Taking the Allies by surprise on December 16th, von Rundstedt launched the famous push through the American V and III Corps in the Ardennes with the object of re-occupying Antwerp to prevent its full utilisation by the Allies as a supply port. Initial gains in this "Battle of the Bulge" were spectacular by the four German armies concerned, an important factor in their favour being the terrible weather which grounded much of 2nd TAF and US 9th TAF. Indeed, it was not until the 22nd that 485 Squadron was able to render any assistance to the hard-pressed Americans.

On several of these *Sweeps* and escort duties over the Ardennes V-2 rockets were observed ascending, and for the first time German jet aircraft were seen. Although the Spitfires "had a go" only on one occasion did W/Cdr Harries, while leading the Squadron as target cover for Bomber Command Lancasters and Halifaxes, claim strikes on an Me 262.

F/O Russell Clarke DFC with OU-U "Kainui" *(Clarke)*.

NH 604, OU-U, taking off from Maldegem, November or December 1944 *(Humphrey)*.

P/O Russell Clarke recalls one of these brief encounters. "The Squadron was proceeding to the target area in open battle formation. We are not proud of the fact that after seeking for some months for German aircraft in the air, our reaction when one in fact sought us was less than professional.

"He came from above and behind and made one swift pass. He did not open fire, or stop to engage, but continued on and down at a speed we couldn't hope to match (although we tried). The CO had seen him closing in and gave the order to 'break' which we did in a rather undisciplined fashion, transforming our erstwhile tidy formation into rather a shambles. Presumably none of us presented him with a target he could utilise at the speed he was making. Whatever his intentions, the immediate effect for each of us was an empty sky, empty not only of Me 262s (happily) but also of Spitfires (embarrassingly), a phenomenon which pilots know about but can't explain."

At this point the records of ML 407's operational life become ambiguous. The aircraft's "Movement Card" which logs each unit with which an individual machine served, states that ML 407 was transferred to 341 (FF) Squadron in 145 Wing on December 28th. This is supported by the entries in 341 Squadron's Operations Record Book which picks up the thread on 29th right on cue. However, these records are contradicted by 485 Squadron's ORB which records a further four operational sorties credited to ML 407 up to the end of the month. There is no way to be certain which is right, although on balance it seems best to follow the "Movement Card" as it is unlikely that the new squadron would record the serial number of an aircraft which it did not possess, whereas the squadron which had flown an "OU-V" with the serial ML 407 for nine months could conceivably continue for a few days after its transfer to refer to its replacement (also coded OU-V) by the same serial number.

If then it is accepted that ML 407 left her first squadron on December 28th, her last pilot with 485 Squadron was Athol Downer. In the nine months she had been with 485 Squadron she had flown the following operations:

Escort Duty:

57 sorties
(US 9th Tactical Air Force: B-26 Marauders. RAF 2nd TAF, 2 Group: Bostons and Mitchells. RAF Bomber Command: Lancasters and Halifaxes. Own Squadron's dive-bombing Spitfires. Targets: *Noball*, road and rail, *Interdiction*, POL dumps etc.).

Dive-Bombing:

31 sorties
(One 500-pound bomb against *Noball* sites and in support of Canadian First Army after D-Day on the Continent).

Beach Patrol:

32 sorties
(British Sector of *Neptune Beach* — the cross-channel assault phase of Operation *Overlord*) During this period $1^{1/4}$ Ju 88s and two Bf 109s claimed destroyed and one damaged, according to Johnnie Houlton).

Sweeps and Armed Recces:

14 sorties
(Principally Interdiction in support of Canadian First Army after D-Day on the Continent).

Shipping Patrols:

4 Sorties
(During *Neptune* and invasion of the Dutch Islands).

Nickelling Raid:

1 Sortie
(Dropping leaflets on Dunkirk).

139 sorties in total
217 hours 50 minutes

LACs Vic strange and Pete Bradley with ML 407 ".. taken on a terrible windy day, waiting to fill up with petrol." Maldegem, December 1944 *(Strange)*.

341 (Free French) Squadron
145 Wing, 84 Group, 2nd TAF, at B.70 Antwerp/Deurne

341 Sqd pilots	ops. in ML 407
Sgt C. Alépée	1
Sgt J. Dabos	3

Sgt Claude Alépée, Schijncel, April 1945 *(Dabos)*.

It was the move from 485 Squadron at this moment which more than anything else preserved ML 407 from almost certain destruction, at least by the *Luftwaffe* – and the transfer itself was the result of a singular stroke of fate. Lying close to the immensely strategic port of Antwerp, the airfield at Deurne, like the city, suffered from numerous attacks by V-1 flying bombs and V-2 rockets. Between December 1944 and March 1945, some 1,265 V-2s and 2,448 V-1s hit Antwerp (compared to 517 and 2,419 respectively received by London).

December 20th, 1944 at B.70 Antwerp/Deurne. After a direct hit by a V-2 on the dispersal area, ML 407 replaced one of the 19 aircraft destroyed *(Alpépée)*.

At about 16.15 hours on December 20th a V-2 rocket hit the dispersal area of 341 Squadron, wiping out 19 of the Squadron's Spitfires. For the next few days those operations which were possible, despite the prevailing misty weather, were mounted with borrowed aircraft from other units of 145 Wing at Deurne. 329, 345 and 74 Squadrons all loaned machines. ML 407 was transferred from 135 Wing to 145 Wing on December 28th and allotted to 341 (Free French) Squadron where she took up the codes "NL-D." Like the other aircraft of the Squadron she was probably decorated with the Croix de Lorraine, just forward of the cockpit door on her port side.

Next day Sgt Claude Alépée flew ML 407, NL-D, as "Blue Two" on a squadron-strength *Fighter Sweep* over the Ardennes battleground in the area of Köln and Koblenz. No enemy aircraft were encountered by the Squadron, but they were

Sgt Claude Alépée, joined the Free French forces in Egypt in 1942 (his father was with the Suez Canal Company) and later sailed round the Cape of Good Hope to Britain where he arrived in August. Basic training was in England, and Service training In Canada, where he won RAF and French "Wings" in February 1943. After operational training in England he joined 341 Squadron from 84 GSU (the operational pilot and aircraft pool for 84 Group, 2nd TAF) in August 1944. He remained on operations until the end of the war in Europe when he returned to Egypt and the Canal Company *(Alpépée)*

ML 407 may have carried Johnny Dabos' yellow baby mascot on the port cowling forward of the wing root.

attacked by a formation of Mustangs and on returning to base found a V-1 flying-bomb "in the circuit" which was also being fired upon by the anti-aircraft guns of their airfield defence. Nevertheless the Operations Record Book laconically records "...the Squadron returned to base without incident..."

Aircraft bearing the identity NL-D usually became the "property" of Sgt Jean "Johnny" Dabos, the youngest member of the Squadron. So two days later it was he who took her up beyond Twente and into Germany towards Osnabrük. It was the 341's penultimate operation of the year, but Johnny Dabos' Log Book records another 40-minute sortie in NL-D on the last day of 1944, "Fighter Sweep DNCO" (Duty Not Carried Out), which was obviously aborted for some reason.

Bodenplatte: January 1st 1945

New Year's day dawned slightly hazy and bitterly cold, the runway at Deurne being icy and unuseable. At about 09.20 the airfield was attacked by a large force of enemy fighters, principally Messerschmitt Bf 109s of *Jagdgeschwader* 77 led by *Major* Erich Leie. Johnny Dabos remembers,

"We were 'at readiness' in the early morning of New Year's Day. Our pilots' room had been installed on the first floor of a wrecked house on the edge of our dispersal area, against the side of a large hangar. We were, as usual, fully equipped for a five minute take-off, our aircraft already fitted with a 500-pound bomb, and waiting for our target to be announced. I was with my old friend Jimmy Davies, deputy Flight Commander of "B" Flight (I was deputy Flight Commander of "A" Flight).

"Then, at some time between 9 and 10 am we heard, all at once, a lot of aircraft beating up the field. As they were firing, we had no doubt about their nationality, and we had the feeling that there were hundreds of them, due to the loudness of the "show". They were Me 109s, Fw 190s and other aircraft we had never seen before. It was wonderful.

"Jimmy and I jumped down the stairs and tried to run to our aircraft with the definite intention of taking-off, whatever happened. But the ground was icy and terribly slippery and we had not far to go before we were on our 'asses'. We lost enough time for the Jerries to turn around and make another fly-by. As we were directly in the line-of-fire of one Messerschmitt we jumped under the hangar and sheltered behind a big box. We were not hit, but when the 109 had gone, we could read on the box alongside us "HANDLE WITH CARE – EXPLOSIVES". At last we got into our aircraft, released the bombs on the ground, and took-off. Too late, they had gone and all we could hear on the R/T were those lucky bastards of Canadians and Poles who were claiming so many aircraft destroyed. We had missed the last fighter battle of the war!"

Sergeant Jean Dabos

Jean Dabos escaped from France in 1939 through Morocco, from where he travelled to England via South America and Canada. On arrival in London, in September 1941, he joined the Free French Air Force at its Headquarters in Carlton Gardens, subsequently finding himself in Scarborough for initial training. Elementary flying training took him to 6 EFTS at Sywell on de Havilland DH.82, Tiger Moth, and overseas again to 31 EFTS De Winton, in Canada. Moving on to the North American Harvard he gained his "Wings" (both RAF and French) at 34 SFTS Medicine Hat, returning to England for advanced flying on Miles Masters at 5 AFU Ternhill. At 57 OTU he was introduced to the Spitfire and joined 341 Squadron at 145 Airfield, Tangmere Sector, in the Spring of 1944.

After moving to the Continent in the wake of Overlord, 341 went over to *Armed Recces*, and on September 28th Sgt Dabos destroyed a Messerschmitt Bf 109, but on November 26th, he was shot-down himself, counting 52 holes in his Spitfire. He later sank a 12,000-ton flak ship with a direct hit in a dive-bombing attack. At the end of the war he was awarded the Légion d'Honneur, Médaille Militaire and the Croix de Guerre.

After the war Dabos became a civil airline pilot, flying Douglas Dakotas, and Sud-Aviation Caravelles. Later he joined Aérospatiale as a test pilot on Caravelles, the Consortium Airbus and Concorde.

Sgt Jean Dabos in April 1945. His Spitfire bears the arms of Alsace *(Alépée)*.

Sgt Christinacce of 341 (Free French) Squadron, Wevelgem, October 1944 *"Alépée)*.

The assault was part of the co-ordinated effort code-named *Bodenplatte*, in which the *Luftwaffe* fielded some 800-900 fighters and intended to surprise the Allied Expeditionary Air Force on the ground. It was to have been a single mighty blow in support of the Ardennes Offensive, hitting the British 2nd TAF and American 9th TAF all over Belgium and Holland. The German aircraft, flying at "zero" feet and often by circuitous routes, took off from their bases before dawn, led by navigating night-fighters. Complete radio silence was observed, and even the FuC 25 identification transmitters had been removed. Indeed such was the secrecy of the operation that many *Luftwaffe* machines were lost to their own flak en route to the targets.

Luckily for ML 407 the assault on Deurne was not well executed. Of the 100-plus fighters which set out, only about 30 actually carried out an attack on the target. The frustrated RAF pilots, grounded by the icy conditions were not impressed by the disorganised gaggles of fighters milling about over Deurne and criticised the evident lack of skill of the German pilots. While *Major* Leie himself was a veteran of 1940, with more than 100 "kills" to his credit and the Knight's Cross with Oak Leaves, many of his pilots were indeed extremely young, ill-trained and with little combat experience.

The terrible losses sustained by the *Luftwaffe* since the summer of 1943 and the policy of continuous, uninterrupted operational service for aircrew, made the loss

"Strategy For Defeat. The Luftwaffe 1933-1945" Williamson Murray (Airpower Research Institute 1983).

of experienced pilots almost inevitable. With the ever-escalating attrition of pilots outstripping the production of aircraft, replacement aircrew were rushed through training and into the operational units, to fill brand new cockpits before they were ready to handle the aircraft efficiently. It has been said that since the early part of 1943 (when German losses of aircraft through non-combatant accidents was on a par with combat losses) the subsequent improvement in accident figures was not so much a result of improved flying safety, but more "the probability that Allied flyers in their overwhelming numbers, were shooting down German pilots before they could crash their aircraft".

It was not until 10.12 hours that 341 Squadron could be scrambled in response to the attack, and by that time nothing was to be seen of the enemy. Following-up after lunch with a Sweep in the area of Enschede and Rheine the result was equally uneventful. However, at 20.00 hours the day ended with another bang when a V-1 fell on the eastern end of the airfield. During the morning's attack the two RAF Wings at Deurne (145 Wing with four Spitfire squadrons and 146 with five Typhoon squadrons) lost only one Typhoon destroyed and 10 damaged. *JG77*, who carried out the attack, lost six pilots killed and four missing (taken prisoner) as a result of AA fire over the target area and on the return journey.

The *Luftwaffe* did not make such a poor showing everywhere. 485 Squadron, from which ML 407 had so recently and fortuitously been transferred, lost 11 Spitfires destroyed and two damaged beyond repair, when *III/JG1* surprised 135 Wing's airfield. This left them with only five serviceable aircraft. *Had ML 407 still been standing on Maldegem airfield that morning, she would almost certainly have been destroyed.*

On January 5th, 341 Squadron was released from operations pending rest and re-equipment with the Spitfire Mk XVI at Turnhouse, in Scotland, but bad weather actually kept them in Belgium until the end of the month.

ML 407 was not however, due for a rest, and was drafted into another squadron, this time 308 (Polish). In the week that ML 407 flew with 341 Squadron she had flown the following operations:

Fighter Sweeps:
3 sorties (Ardennes)

Scramble:
1 sortie (*Bodenplatte*)

4 sorties in total
6 hours 15 minutes

The fate that might so easily have overtaken ML 407 on January 1st 1945, at B.65 Maldegem. The Luftwaffe attack left 485 Squadron with only five serviceable aircraft. F/O Al Roberts (below) and F/O Don Taylor (above) contemplate the remains of their Spitfires *(Clarke)*.

308 (Polish) Squadron
131 Wing, 84 Group, 2nd TAF, at B.61 (Gent)

January 1st, 1945, B.61 St Denijs Westrem, Gent. Aircraft and vehicles of 131 Wing blaze after the *Luftwaffe* attack *(Polish Institute and Sikorski Museum)*.

308 Sqd pilots	ops. in ML 407
W/O J. Sawoszczyk	1
F/O W. Stanski	1

On January 4th 1945, ML 407 left 341 Squadron, 145 Wing and joined 131 Wing at B.61 St Denijs Westrem, near Gent. She was one of six replacements delivered that day for losses sustained by 308 Squadron when *II/JG1* (part of the same *Jagdgeschwader* which hit 485 Squadron at Maldegem) attacked on New Year's Day (although she was not officially taken on charge by the Squadron until the 11th). Eleven Spitfires were lost, six on the ground, four crash-landed from fuel shortage after combat over the field and one was shot down. 302 Squadron, 317 Squadron and 316 Squadron of the same Polish Wing also lost 18 Spitfires between

F/Lt J Mierzejewski and his ground-crew of 308 (Polish) Squadron at Gent, Belgium, October 10th 1944. Note the Polish ensign on the cowling, and that Spitfire MJ 342, ZF-B, is carrying two 250-pound and one 500-pound bomb (Mierzejewski).

them, for the loss of two pilots killed. It was even more disastrous for *II/JG1* however, because the Polish Wing was on its way home from various early-morning operations and arrived over the airfield at about the same time that the attack was in full swing. *JG1* lost a total of 24 pilots killed and missing during *Bodenplatte*, most of them to the highly trained and aggressive Polish pilots.

On January 3rd, HQ 2nd TAF decreed that all 2nd TAF aircraft must carry the red, white, blue and yellow "C"-type roundel on the fuselage and upper and lower wing-surfaces. In addition, the sky fuselage band was to be removed, and propeller spinners painted black. All remnants of the black-and-white "invasion stripes" were to be eradicated. ML 407 would have been no exception to the rule. The intention was to increase the impact of the national markings, as American aircrew and gunners were constantly attacking British aircraft. The dull red and blue upper wing-surface markings of British aircraft were difficult to distinguish in the heat of combat and at this time German aircraft wore minimal black or dark-green crosses, and had adopted "defence of the Reich" fuselage bands in much the same position as the British day-fighter's "sky" fuselage band. All this, compounded by the exuberance and lack of type-recognition skills prevalent with our Ally, precipitated many dangerous encounters.

January was a month of very poor weather and 14 days were unfit for operations. ML 407 flew only twice with the Squadron operationally (bearing the

Flying Officer Waclaw Stanski VM, DFC, KW and two bars

Spitfire LF Mk IX MJ 342, "ZF-O", damaged by flak on a dive-bombing and strafing operation over the Amersfoort area Netherlands, February 3rd 1945. Stanski's aircraft being unserviceable, he had borrowed this machine, usually flown by S/Ldr Ignacy Olszewski *(Polish Institute and Sikorski Museum)*.

Waclaw Stanski was born in 1920, in Bezenczuk, then in Russia. His family returned to Siedlece in Poland, when it became independent and he grew up longing to be a pilot. While at senior school young Waclaw Stanski had already attended a spare-time course for would-be pilots at the Deblin flying school, where youngsters were introduced to gliding and parachuting. On leaving his gimnazjum in the summer of 1939 he opted for military training at Swidnik, with the Air Force specifically in mind. On September 1st the German army crossed the frontier of Poland without any formal declaration of war and the world learned the meaning of the word *Blitzkrieg* –

"lightning war". With the inevitable fall of his gallant country, Stanski left to continue fighting abroad. He eventually arrived in England, via Romania, Bulgaria, Libya and France, where he joined the RAF.

After the usual training schedule he was posted to 308 Squadron, 131 (Polish) Wing, at Northolt on December 12th 1942. He went into action in the Spitfire Mk Vb, and during the next year flew *Rhubarbs*, *Lag* operations (decoy formations), fighter affiliation (with 4 Group Halifaxes, *Ramrods*, *Roadsteads* and bomber escorts. In early 1944 the Squadron began bombing training, which it put into practice on the near-Continent in May. During the D-Day period 308 Squadron did its share of *Beach Patrols*, then returned to bombing and *Armed-Recces* as the armies moved on. In the winter of 1944-45 the accent was on dive-bombing V-2 sites. The Squadron shot down 12 1/2 enemy aircraft on January 1st, for the loss of one pilot. He was F/O Waclaw Chojnacki who was flying ZF-P, instead of its usual pilot, his friend Waclaw Stanski.

Stanski claimed 2 1/2 aerial victories between 1942 and '45 and ended his service in 1946 when the Squadron disbanded at Ahlhorn, as a Flight Lieutenant Virtuti Militari (5th class), DFC and Cross of Valour with two bars.

In February 1947 "he put his medals in his pocket" and returned to Poland.

Despite a period of repression doing enforced manual labour in the late '40s and the '50s, he managed to keep flying for most of his life, gliding, as a parachute-jump pilot, an inspector of aircraft training, flight-instructing youngsters, helping re-establish and teach aerobatics (becoming a competition-judge), and managing a number of Polish sports-flying clubs. He participated in World Championships in Russia, Czechoslovakia and the USA and gained a national silver medal for gliding in 1961. He was also the first Polish civilian to fly the massive Antonov An-2 biplane transport.

He wrote, "I am pleased with my work, it is a pleasure to watch a growing band of pilots, particularly as they are all young, our group (meaning the wartime generation) gets smaller at a terrifying rate." Stanski died in Plock in 1986 shortly after learning a Spitfire he once flew, ML 407, was back in the air.

At Grimbergen, Belgium, F/O Waclaw Stanski of 308 (Polish) Squadron and his rigger examine wing damage sustained by his Spitfire LF Mk IXe MJ 342, ZF-O, on the dive-bombing and strafing sortie over the Amersfoort area, Netherlands on February 3rd 1945 *(Polish Institute and Sikorski Museum)*.

B.60 Grimbergen, near the only substantial buildings on the field. The Spitfires now have black spinners, no rear fuselage identification band and red, white, blue and yellow roundels both on upper and lower wing-surfaces. A 45-gallon long-range slipper-tank lies in the snow, and the Spitfire beyond is carrying two 250-pound bombs under its wings and a 500-pound bomb under the centre-section *(Polish Institute and Sikorski Museum)*.

code letters ZF-R), first on January 22nd, with F/O Waclaw Stanski on an *Armed Weather Recce* taking in Nijmegen, Apeldoorn, Zwolle, Zuider Zee and Utrecht and second on the 24th, with W/O Jozef Sawoszczyk during which barges were attacked with 250-pound under-wing bombs by sections of Spitfires. One direct hit was scored. Both these sorties were out of B.60 Grimbergen, near Brussels, to which 131 Wing moved on January 14th.

In the month ML 407 had been with 308 Squadron she had flown the following operations:

Armed Weather Recce:

1 sortie

Anti-Shipping:

1 sortie

2 sorties in total
2 hours 45 minutes

ML 407, ZF-R, in the deep snow of January 1945 at St Denijs Westrem (Gent) *(Sawoszczyk)*.

Warrant Officer Jozef Sawoszczyk KW and two bars

Jozef Sawoszczyk as a F/Sgt at B.61 Gent, 1944. The Spitfire is ML 323, ZF-S *(Sawoszczyk)*.

W/O Jozef Sawoszczyk was born in Nowogrodek, Poland, now Bialo in Russia. In 1938, as a seventeen year-old, he joined the Polish school for NCO pilots at Swiecie, but his training was interrupted next year by the German invasion when the school was evacuated. With the help of the Polish Embassy Sawoszczyk escaped from a camp in Romania, and travelled to Lyon, France where he was posted as a munitions and petrol guard. When France fell in July 1940, the NCO school evacuated again, to England, where he was able to complete his flying training and gained his "Wings" in 1942.

In January 1944 he joined 308 (Polish) Squadron at Northolt, and stayed on its strength until March 1945, completing 141 operational sorties, 30 of them strafing and 41 dive-bombing attacks, during which he released 28,000 pounds of bombs on the enemy and destroyed numerous transport targets. On January 24th 1945 he flew Spitfire ML 407, ZF-R on his 124th operation and destroyed a barge at Hellevoetsluis with one 500-pound bomb.

In May 1945 Sawoszczyk joined 595 Squadron at Aberporth, and in June 16 (P)SFTS, Newton. His decorations include the Polish Cross of Valour, 1, 2, and 3. In 1948 he emigrated to Argentina and in 1958, the USA.

349 (Belgian) Squadron
135 Wing, 84 Group, 2nd TAF, at B.77 Gilze-Rijen

Spitfire LF Mk XVIe TB 991, GE-L, 1945. Note the yellow outer ring around the wing roundel (Seydel).

349 Sqd pilots	ops. in ML 407
F/Sgt L. Branders	1
F/Lt A. Claesen	5
F/Sgt A. van Hamme	1
F/Lt G. Seydel	1
F/Sgt D. Smerdon	1
F/O S. Tuck	1

For several weeks the Allied Air Force had been engaged in wide-ranging concentrated attacks on the supply-lines, railways, bridges and headquarters of the enemy, in the rear of the next battle-ground. The code-name of the imminent offensive was *Veritable*, its object being to clear General Schlemm's First Para Army from the area between the river Maas and the Rhine. General Crerar was in overall command of Canadian II Corps and British XXX Corps. Virtually the whole of 2nd TAF was to be engaged in the operation, with the light and medium bombers of US 9th Air Force, and the heavy bombers of Bomber Command and US 8th Air Force on call when needed.

Veritable

Fifteen days after her last sortie with 308 Squadron ML 407 was on active service with 349 (Belgian) Squadron, wearing the identification letters GE-P.

By now the most forward positions were on the river Maas (which in France is known as the Meuse). From Roermond, in the south-east panhandle of Holland, to

In May 1945, 349 Squadron re-equipped with the Spitfire LF Mk XVIe which shared the same type number with the Mk IX (Type 361) and differed only in the Packard built Merlin 266 engine (Seydel).

a point just south of Nijmegen the Maas curves westward to the North Sea. 349 Squadron was based at the established airfield of Gilze Rijen, recently vacated by the *Luftwaffe* and some 10 kilometers inside Holland's border with Belgium and not much further than that from the Maas.

The extremely wet weather persisted, washing-out whole days for flying purposes and keeping the field water-logged. However, on those days which were suitable for operations, the Squadron threw itself vigorously into the job of harrying the German ground forces and their transport. Throughout the first half of February, apart from a couple of bomber escort duties, most of the action was in the form of *Armed Recces* particularly in areas Y and Z. This was a roughly triangular area marked by Rotterdam in the south, Enschede on Holland's eastern border with Germany, and Zwolle to the north.

February 8th was a day of intensive *Armed Recces*, and also the debut of ML 407 with 349 Squadron. Made available to F/Lt "Tony" Claesen, ML 407 took part in the second operation of the day. In the words of the Squadron's Operations Record Book, "this time they really found some transport".

Ten Spitfires, as two units of five, took off at 14.00 and 14.10 hours respectively for area Y, in the vicinity of Deventer and Zwolle. On their return they claimed several locomotives damaged, one destroyed, numerous trucks, two barges, an HDT, and a MET (motorised enemy transport) damaged plus one each of HDT and MET destroyed. ML 407, "P-Peter", was directly involved in the damage of 12 trucks and a locomotive, and the destruction of another loco' and the MET.

"B" Flight 349 Squadron, B.106 Twenthe, April 1945. Back row, L to R: F/O Smith, F/O Sidney Tuck, F/Sgt Eid, F/Lt Antoine Claesen (KIA April 25th 1945), F/Lt Gaby Seydel, F/O Erkes, F/Sgt Donald Smerdon. Kneeling: F/Sgt Delbecq. Front row: F/Sgt Gibbs, F/Lt Mycroft, F/Sgt Léon Branders, F/Sgt Albert Van Hamme, F/O Van de Wale *(Tuck via Banks)*.

F/Sgt Albert Van Hamme

At outbreak of war Albert Van Hamme was a student at Cambridge. On joining the RAF, basic training began in England and service training in Canada. He joined 349 Squadron in February 1945 and remained a regular officer in la Force Aérienne Belge post-war, retiring as a Colonel in 1972 and having flown some 21 different aircraft types *(Van Hamme).*

For the next operation of the day the pilot was F/Sgt Donald Smerdon, one of the few Englishmen to fly ML 407. The five aircraft involved managed to find and damage three barges and a locomotive in the area around Deventer and Zwolle. February 9th followed on in similar style, but this time the Squadron put up 20 sorties, with aircraft operating in pairs throughout the day. On the first of four sorties ML 407, flown by "B" Flight's Commander F/Lt Gaby Seydel with F/O Pierre Erkes as his "number two", accounted for three locomotives and four trucks damaged and a loco' destroyed.

The next incident of the day is best described by F/Sgt Léon Branders, who was "number two" of a pair led by F/Lt Tony Claesen who was flying ML 407. He remembers clearly that on take-off he could not close his cockpit-hood which was reason for a five-minute trip marked in his Log Book, immediately preceding the sortie.

"We flew next on an *Armed Recce* mission in the region of Zwolle. On this occasion we attacked a train. While attacking as 'number one' Tony called me, attracting my attention to a high-tension line on my way down. As I was dodging it, I looked towards the train again, just as it started exploding wagon by wagon. I had nothing else to do but climb up and join my leader. Funnily enough, he never looked back at the train. I imagine he knew he had hit the engine but he must have been worried about me and the high tension line. He would not believe my story after landing. So that's one sortie he did with the P-for-Peter."

The ORB reveals a second locomotive damaged on this sortie, and also a locomotive destroyed by F/Lt Claesen the same day, once more flying ML 407.

The next few days the weather again hampered operations, but on February 13th the Squadron was able to continue its search for enemy transport. F/Sgt Branders was flying ML 407 in the second pair of aircraft to take-off for an *Armed Recce* beyond the Reichswald Forest, which was the toughest battle-ground of Operation *Veritable.*

"Crossing the Reichswald Forest was so hectic (like getting through those little bits of paper people throw at you during carnivals) that we were ordered not to go across low level if we could not get rid of our drop-tank. That day I had to turn back. My leader was Pierre Erkes. The moment I told him I could not get rid of my drop tank and started turning, a gun began shooting at me with tracers. I started down at it, shooting also, but rapidly broke away remembering I still had that drop tank."

Later in the morning ML 407 was airborne again, this time with F/Sgt Van Hamme in company with F/O Erkes in MK 804.

"Our mission was to attack anything which moved in the area Cleve, Emerich, Wezel and Geldern. A great number of German troops were concentrated there,

Flight Lieutenant Gaby Seydel DFC

(Zucker).

Gabriel Seydel began basic flying training in September 1939 at Wevelgem, the Belgian Elementary Flying Training School, beginning on the Avro 504N and continuing with the Stampe et Vertongen SV4 bis. After the German occupation of his country the student pilots of his course left Belgium on a trek which wound-up in Oujda, Morocco.

They left Casablanca for England in August 1940, where he joined the RAF and picked-up his training in November at EFTS Odiham, with the Miles Magister. At 5 SFTS Ternhill his service training progressed to the Miles Master from April 1941, until graduating to 58 OTU Grangemouth for training on operational types – Hurricane I and Spitfire Mk I.

On August 25th 1941, Sgt Seydel was posted to 131 Squadron's Belgian Flights where he stayed until joining 350 (Belgian) Squadron, which was forming at Valley, on November 14th. Equipped with the Spitfire Mk IIa, this first Belgian Squadron became operational in December but the real action began the following April, when it moved to Debden. In *Sweeps* over northern France P/O Seydel had successes against rail, road and river transport, but it was not until Operation *Jubilee* that he claimed 1 1/2 Focke-Wulf Fw 190s damaged on August 19th, 1942. Staying with 350 Squadron until March 1943, he had further successes against transportation across the Channel, before attending Fighter Leader School at Charmydown in May and transferring to 349 (Belgian) Squadron, newly formed at Collyweston on June 7th.

A year later 349 Squadron was over the Normandy beachhead, and on D-Day F/Lt Seydel claimed a share in a damaged Junkers Ju 88, next day damaged a Focke Wulf Fw 190, and on the 8th shared the destruction of a Fw 190. It was not until July 26th that he claimed complete credit for shooting down a Messerschmitt Bf 109 which was part of a mixed formation of more than 30 Messerschmitts and Focke Wulfs which were attacking bombers escorted by 135 Wing. A "rest" with ADGB of four months was followed by a brief return to 350 Squadron at Maldegem, before rejoining 349 where he stayed until just before its transfer from BAFO to the new Belgian Air Force in 1946.

Gaby Seydel's Log Book lists some 24 different types of aircraft flown, including Avro 504N, Stampe SV4, Miles Magister, Master and Martinet, Hawker Hurricane, Typhoon and Tempest, eight Spitfire variants, Avro Lancaster, Republic P-47 Thunderbolt, Auster, de Havilland Dragon Rapide, Fiesler Storch and Gotha.

F/Lt Antoine "Tony" Claesen

Tony Claesen joined the Belgian Air Force at Deurne in September 1939 and by the outbreak of war was flying solo at the Elementary Flying Training School at Wevelgem. On May 10th 1940, the whole of 82éme Course (including Claesen and Gaby Seydel) was withdrawn first to Carpiquet then to Marseilles which it left on the 28th, for North Africa and finished up in Oujda in French Morocco on July 10th. The Belgians left Morocco via Casablanca and arrived at Cardiff in August. It was not until December 1940 that Claesen resumed training, at EFTS Odiham, going on to 5 SFTS Ternhill (Miles Masters and Hawker Hurricanes) in 1941 and eventually being introduced to the Spitfire at 58 OTU Grangemouth. His career continued in the same pattern as his classmate Gaby Seydel's but ended on April 25th 1945 when his Spitfire crashed in an attack on a column of enemy vehicles south of Wesermünde.

F/Sgt Léon Branders

Léon Branders escaped from Belgium to Spain, where he was interned from November 1941 until May 1942. In June he volunteered in Lisbon, arriving by convoy at Loch Ewe later that month. Basic training was in England and Service training in Canada. Operational training in Britain followed the award of "Wings" at 34 SFTS Medicine Hat and he joined 349 Squadron from 84 GSU in August 1944, at 135 Airfield Selsey. He flew operationally until the end of hostilities and stayed with 349 Squadron when it became part of the new Belgian Air Force and was awarded the Croix de Guerre, Palme et Lion and Croix Militaire 1ére Classe. He retired as a Colonel in 1976, after a distinguished career both as a field and staff officer. His Log Book boasts some 33 types from de Havilland DH.82 Tiger Moth through piston and jet fighters to the C.130. NATO staff appointments took him to Washington, the Antarctic and London apart from Brussels. Latterly he became President of the Royal Belgian Aero Club.

defending themselves fiercely. It was their homeland and they had their backs to the Rhine. Flak was so heavy we called the area a flak-nest", remembers Van Hamme.

"Attacking a cluster of motorised enemy transport, we went in very low and had to pull up rather abruptly to avoid flying debris. Suddenly, there and then, my engine cut. Happily my high speed took me just above a layer of low cloud where I could recover my breath and think of a decision. Bail-out? Force-land? What – in that very hostile spot? My R/T, of course, had cut out at the same time so my leader, unaware of what was happening to me, went in for another attack while I just prayed, held on and hoped to hear that engine pick up again. Then it coughed and growled, and with a grinding noise restarted, shuddering.

"I was all alone in the skies by then, except for the tracer-flak chasing me and had taken a south-westerly course. Nursing the engine gently, it kept turning somehow and took me to B.78 Eindhoven, where I landed. Twenty-five unforgettable seconds."

On February 19th, 349 Squadron departed for England, where it was due to convert to Tempests at Predannack. Its Spitfires were left at Gilze-Rijen where the

Training in Canada, 1943-44. Sidney Tuck (later of 349 Squadron), standing third from left with his course-mates at 41 Weyburn, Saskatchewan *(Tuck via Banks)*.

Fairchild Cornell II, 34 EFTS Assiniboia, Saskatchewan *(Tuck via Banks)*.

last remaining 135 Wing component happened to be number 485 (NZ) Squadron! This probably explains why, according to her "Movement Card", ML 407 was transferred again not from 349 but from 485 Squadron to the Free French 145 Wing on February 22nd (which was also the date on which 485 Squadron left to join 349 Squadron at Predannack). So, not for the last time either, ML 407 was once more in the care of the New Zealanders who had been her first "owners", if only for a couple of days.

In the six days that ML 407 had been with 349 Squadron she had flown the following operations:

Armed Recces:

(*Interdiction*)

10 sorties in total
12 hours 45 minutes.

North American Harvard IIB, December 14th 1943, 41 SFTS. Sidney Tuck is in the front seat *(Tuck via Banks)*.

345 (Free French) Squadron

145 Wing, 84 Group, 2nd TAF at B.85 Schijndel

Commandant Accart, winter 1944. In 345 Squadron the CO's Spitfire was normally coded 2Y-A *(Droumatakis)*.

345 Squadron, like 349 Squadron, was operating mainly to the north of the battle area between the Maas and the Rhine and although hampered by more bad weather, the first two weeks after ML 407 joined produced quite a mixed bag of operations. These included *Rail Interdiction*, a direct army-support attack for Canadian II Corps in the Hochwald forest battle (Operation *Blockbuster*, the second phase of *Veritable*), *Armed Recces* against MET and a couple of escort duties for Mitchells which were bombing marshalling yards at Lengerich and Borken, inside Germany to the rear of the defenders.

345 Sqd pilots	ops. in ML 407
Lt F. Boyer de Bouillane	1
Lt M. Gelly	1
Comdt G. Guizard	8
Capt M. Guérin	1
Lt L. Harmel	1
Lt R. Le Boëtté	1
Lt P. Seguy	1

Lt Harmel, Lt Le Maire, Lt René Le Boëtté and Lt Max Gelly of "A" Flight, 345 Squadron *(Le Boëtté)*.

Le Boëtté escaped from Carentec in Brittany in a sailing boat, in May 1943 and landed at Porthleven in Cornwall. Like Boyer de Bouillane he was already a serving officer in L'Armée de l'Air trained at L'Ecole de l'Air in 1938, on the same types of aircraft. He finished the war with 345 Squadron's top score against ground targets, the Croix de Guerre with three Palms and an Officier de la Légion d'Honneur. In 1947 he joined Air France to fly Douglas DC-3 and DC-4, Bloch Kanguedoc, Lockheed Constellation, Sud Aviation Caravelle and Boeing 707.

ML 407 may have carried "La Cigogne" of René Fonck's WWI unit, Spa 103, below the starboard windscreen.

On his return from leave, at the end of February, Commandant Guizard, the CO of 345 Squadron, selected ML 407 as his personal machine. Almost certainly, as was the normal practice on the Squadron, its code letters "2Y-A" which were usually applied to the CO's aircraft were painted on either side of the French Air Force roundel on the fuselage, and French rudder stripes replaced RAF fin flashes. Once more the Croix de Lorraine was displayed alongside the cockpit door.

After lunch on March 5th Comdt Guizard led his Squadron back to England, bound for Tangmere, but was diverted to Manston by foul weather. The next two weeks were spent in armament practice at Fairwood Common, before returning to Schijndel on April 2nd, after more bad-weather delays.

While in England the Squadron strength was restored to full complement, as four pilots had been lost in February. In the first months of 1945 and as the perimeter of German defence shrank, so there was a consequent concentration of light flak guns as units were pulled-back into the defensive circle. The result of this was a marked increase in the loss-rates of 2nd TAF squadrons engaged in ground-attack work.

With the crossing of the Rhine, by Canadian II Corps at Emmerich and Rees, 345 Squadron became almost fully engaged striking at transport ahead of the rapid advance, which by the 28th had taken Leeuwarden in the north of Holland, via Zutphen, Deventer and Zwolle. ML 407 took an active part in all of this, flown by several different pilots. But on April 13th 345 Squadron began to re-equip with Spitfire XVIs and that was also the day on which ML 407 flew her last sortie as 2Y-A.

".. . in the afternoon the Squadron was ordered to get the maximum number of aircraft airborne to bomb a concentration of 800 troops at Vecht, west of

Commandant Gaston Guizard DFC

(Droumatakis).

Gaston Guizard was born in a little town in the South of France, called Pézenas, the son of an army General. He joined L'Armée de l'Air through the Ecole de Saint Cyr.

In 1943 in Saragoza, while escaping from occupied France through Spain, he met Jean Accart who was to become the first Commanding Officer of 345 Squadron. Commandant Accart named Capitaine Guizard as his deputy when 345 Squadron was conceived in North Africa, and the nucleus of the new squadron left Algiers on January 28th 1944, abroad SS *Strathmore*.

Guizard was responsible for the destruction of at least one enemy aircraft during the 21-month existence of the Squadron. He took over command of 345 Squadron in October 1944, until its disbandment in November 1945. His decorations included the DFC, Officier de la Légion d'Honneur and Croix de Guerre with five Palms.

From July to December 1946 Guizard served in Indo-China, from which conflict he emerged with the Croix de Guerre Far East. For the next three years he was with SHAPE (Supreme Headquarters Allied Powers Europe), Versailles, and from 1950-54 commanded L'Ecole de Guerre. Promoted to Colonel in 1954, he commanded the Base Aérienne Luxeuil which he left in 1957 for Allied Headquarters, Fontainebleau.

In 1959 he was placed in command of 5th Division, Algiers and it was in Algeria on September 16th 1960, that he, with 10 other officers, was killed when their Nord 2500 crashed on a secret night mission.

Pilots of 345 Squadron. Late summer 1944. Left to right: Lt Kerourio, Capt Remy, Comdt Accart, Capt Jacquement, Capt Guizard, Lt Decroo, Lt Harmel, Lt Seguy, Lt Mareshchal de Longeville, Unknown. Note battle damage to engine cowling and fuel tank cover (Accart).

Capt Maurice Guérin DFC MBE (standing) and Lt Félix Boyer de Bouillane. Guérin, deputy "B" Flight Commander, was selected in 1943, to join 345 Squadron from L'Ecole de l'Air Marrakesh. In 1952 he was killed when his Vampire crashed near Mont de Marsan.

Boyer de Bouillane stayed in L'Armée de l'Air until 1968. His service included Indo China War 1951-53, Air Attaché Saigon 1959-62 and Armed Forces Attaché Stockholm 1965-68. His Log Book includes Morane 315 and 230, Caudron Simoun and Goëland, Potez 63, Leo 45, Curtiss P-36, Republic P-47 Thunderbolt, Grumman F8F Bearcat, Lockheed T-33 and Dassault 315. He retired a Colonel.

Deventer. All bombs fell in the target area and the troops were well and truly strafed. Three houses were left burning fiercely. We had three aircraft damaged by flak," reported the Squadron ORB.

In the six weeks that ML 407 had been with 345 Squadron she had flown the following operations:

Armed Recces:

8 sorties (disruption of MET ahead of Canadian II Corps advance)

Army Support:

1 sortie (Hochwald Forest area of *"Blockbuster"*)

Interdiction:

3 sorties (rail targets central Holland)

Escort Duty:

2 sorties (Mitchells bombing marshalling yards in Germany beyond the Rhine defences)

14 sorties in total
17 hours 55 minutes.

332 (Norwegian) Squadron
132 Wing, 84 Group, 2nd TAF at B.85 Schijndel

332 Sqd pilots	ops. in ML 407
Sgt R. Anonsen	2
Lt J. Roesland	1
Sgt E. Stigset	2

Sharing the airfield at Schijndel with 145 Wing were the squadrons of 132 Wing, and it was to one of the latter, 332 (Norwegian), that ML 407 passed when the Mk IXs of 345 Squadron were exchanged for Mk XVI Spitfires.

The Norwegians were engaged upon a similar programme of operations to that of the French, *Armed Recces* ahead of the swiftly moving Canadians who were advancing through central Holland to the north-west. Targets included anything which looked like enemy transport that moved on road, rail or water. During the month casualties began to mount up, three pilots killed including the CO Major Bolstad (who was the only Norwegian pilot to shoot-down a Me 262), and seven Spitfires lost to intense light flak.

ML 407 joined 332 Squadron at Schijndel on April 16th, but on 18th the Squadron was relocated close to the German Frontier at B.106 Twenthe, near Enschede. From there, on the 19th, three pilots of 332 Squadron each did sorties over the Frisian Islands with ML 407, now identified by the code letters AH-B. These included a Report On Shipping and Armed Recces.

Ranging from Borkum to Wilhelmshaven the Squadron made the following claims: 1 APV (armoured patrol vehicle) damaged, 1 bus destroyed, 1 MET destroyed, 1 MET and trailer damaged, 1 staff car strafed N.R.O. (No Results Observed), 1 M/C (Motorcycle) destroyed, 1 large patrol boat, 1 tug, 1 large vessel all strafed, stopped and several strikes seen in each case. With no casualties to themselves, the results were rated as good.

It was to fall to Sgt Egil Stigset to fly the last recorded operational sortie of ML 407's war. On April 21st 1945, at 18.30 hours in the company of PL 138, AH-R, flown by Lt Kolling, she took off on one last *Armed Recce*, "Amsterdam area, on the deck". The flight lasted 1 1/4 hours, landing back at 19.45 hours at Twenthe. Whatever target presented itself "duly received attention" but MET activity was

B.85 Schijndel on April 16th or 17th, 1945. 332 Squadron dispersal area, including Spitfire AH-B which, chronologically, should be ML 407 *(Stigset).*

Sgt Ronald Anonsen

Ronald Anonsen (no photo) volunteered in 1942 for RNAF being a Canadian of Norwegian descent. Trained in Little Norway he got his "Wings" in May 1944, and joined 332 Squadron at Schijndel in time to collect an 88 mm flak shell in his port wing over Wilhelmshaven. Discharged in 1945 in Norway, he joined the RCAF during the early '50s and after a five-year commission turned to bush flying in Newfoundland and Labrador, which included mail delivery, ambulance service, forest fire patrol and extinguishing *(Anonsen)*.

very limited, although there were considerable numbers of cyclists and HDT to be seen.

Next day 332 Squadron was withdrawn from operations and transferred to Fighter Command, flying to Dyce in Scotland en route home to Norway, where it was (with 331 Squadron) to form the nucleus of the new Norwegian Air Force.

In the week that ML 407 had been with 332 Squadron she had flown the following operations:

Armed Recces:

2 sorties (Central and N.W. Holland)

Recce/Report on Shipping:

3 sorties (Frisian Islands)

5 sorties in total
7 hours 15 minutes.

Major Johannes Roesland in 1983 with Norwegian Armed Forces Museum's Spitfire LF Mk IX MH 350.

Johannes Roesland escaped from Norway in a small fishing boat in August 1941. His flying training was in Little Norway and Moose Jaw, Canada, where he won his "Wings" in October 1942. April 1943 found him with 332 Squadron at North Weald and he stayed with the Squadron until 1946. During this time he shared in the destruction of a Messerschmitt Bf 109E and a Me 410 Hornisse. After demobilisation he joined the airline ONL (SAS) briefly, to fly Lockheed Lodestars and Douglas DC-3 Dakotas, but left to go into business. From 1976 he held senior positions in RAFA (Royal Air Force Association) and was elected Life Vice President of the Norwegian Branch.

Incredibly, the Spitfire beside which Major Roesland is standing in the picture above, MH 350, was one of the predecessors of ML 407 as Johnnie Houlton's personal aircraft. MH 350 joined 485 (NZ) Squadron on August 8th 1943 and left on June 15th 1944. Throughout its operational life with the Squadron it was also "OU-V". On August 27th 1943 Houlton destroyed a Fw 190 and on September 16th shared a Fw 190 destroyed and damaged two Bf 109s in this aircraft. For the full story see *"Spitfire Strikes"* by Johnnie Houlton (John Murray 1985) pp 125-128 pp 134-136 *(Erling Gjoesund)*.

Sergeant Egil Stigset

Sgt Egil Stigset, apparently wearing an USAAF A-2 flying jacket, at B.85 Schijndel ("Bulldozers and PSP") on April 16th or 17th 1945. Spitfire AH-B, third from the right is probably ML 407 *(Stigset)*.

Egil Stigset left Norway in response to the Norwegian Government's BBC appeal for volunteers to join the "free" forces abroad. He travelled to Stockholm, where a Norwegian military aircraft was waiting to ferry volunteers to Leuchars, in Scotland. Once in Britain he joined the Royal Norwegian Air Force. Having completed his basic flying training he was posted to 5 AFU Tern Hill from September 1944 to January '45 and to 57 OTU Eshott from February to March for operational training. Next month he joined 84 GSU Lasham, which was an establishment created for 2nd TAF in order to maintain a pool of both operational aircrew and aircraft to supply the squadrons in the field.

He did not linger at Lasham very long however, joining 332 Squadron at 132 Wing airfield, B.85 Schijndel, on April 14th.

Schijndel, he discovered, "was a temporary airfield constructed for the occasion by the engineers (Bulldozers and Pierced Steel Planking or PSP)" and after a local flight in formation he made a second *Local Recce* in Spitfire ML 407, AH-B, to familiarise himself with the area, returning after 1½ hours. He flew on each of the remaining five days of 332 Squadron's operational life in 2nd TAF and on April 21st 1945, also had the honour of flying ML 407 on her last recorded operational sortie of WWII.

Next day 332 Squadron was transferred to ADGB and subsequently Sgt Stigset flew home to Norway, via Dyce. He remained in general duties, fighter aircraft (single engined) adding de Havilland Vampire, North American F-86G and F-86F, Northrop F-5 (two-seat) and General Dynamics F-16 (two-seat) to his list of types, plus training and transport aircraft. In 1982 he retired as a Colonel in the Royal Norwegian Air Force.

Return to 485 Squadron
132 Wing, 84 Group, 2nd TAF at B.106 Twenthe

Haircut, 2nd TAF-style, 1945 *(Edwards)*.

Armourer Eddie Platten, of 485 Squadron, writing home from his quarters at Twenthe, April 1945 (Edwards).

("Memoirs of the War")

Withdrawn to UK to convert to Tempests, which were swiftly replaced by Typhoons, due to shortages, 485 Squadron had been at Predannack since February. But in April they were back in Holland again, though with no aircraft of their own.

"Left England for the Continent for the second time about April 12th. Lay off Southend pier a day and a night. Felt rather homesick. Sailed at 8 am and arrived Ostend 2.30 pm, calm sea and a wizard day. No activity until within sight of Belgian coast when the hun sank a tanker – hell of a fire.

"Left Ostend for Blankenberge and arrived in time for tea. The place has changed in the few weeks since we were there last. The shops are brighter and fuller, and already they have started decorating and clearing up, nothing but beer in the cafes though.

485 Squadron armourer Derek "Slim" Edwards atop one of the deadly German 88 mm anti-aircraft guns at Twenthe, April 1945 *(Edwards)*.

* There is an unconfirmed reference to ML 407 appearing as SK-N of 165 Squadron in June 1944. The author has been unable to trace the aeroplane in that Squadron at any time (so far). The only possible connection of ML 407 to this ADGB squadron is that 165 Squadron was at Dyce when 332 Squadron arrived there from the Continent in April 1945, and subsequently both squadrons flew Spitfire IXs to Norway, 165 Squadron returning to UK in September. Countering this scenario is the evidence of ML 407's "Movement Card' which records the return of ML 407 to 485 Squadron as explained above.

Like ML 407, Max Collett"s Spitfire NH 519, OU-D, "Waipawa Special III", was taken over by 485 Squadron from 332 (Norwegian) Squadron on arrival at Twenthe in April 1945. Note the black spinner and lack of a fuselage band, which were changes made in January to the markings of all 2nd TAF aircraft. It would also have a yellow ring around both upper and lower wing-surface roundels. NH 519 was AH-D with 332 Squadron and it seems that only the squadron code was changed when the aircraft joined 485 Squadron. By this token, ML 407 which was AH-B would almost certainly become OU-E *(Collett)*.

" Left at 7 am for 135 Wing in Bedford troop carriers and arrived north-east of Nijmegen about 12 hours later. Stayed the night – poor food and heavy gunfire all night; didn't sleep much. Rolled out in the morning again for 132 Wing at Enschede – hell of a journey, lost our way skirting enemy 'pocket' and were in enemy territory four times. Crossed the Rhine near Cleves, passed through several other towns too while in Germany – all in ruins and stinking like hell from burst sewers. Arrived at Enschede in northern Holland at dinner time and had the lousiest meal of all time. We only stayed here at 132 about a week relieving the 'Norge' Squadron – the food was absolutely starvation diet: hard biscuits and a stew or marg', meal after meal, no mail or cigarettes, and everyone was glad when we left."

Nevertheless with typical New Zealand initiative, 485 fixed up a deal with the Norwegians (who were about to emplane for Dyce) to take over their Spitfires which were standing around on dispersal. ML 407 was of course one of those machines, and so it returned to its first squadron.

Joe Roddis adds, "We picked up a full complement of Spits left behind by the departing unit and soon had them to our liking. We painted the OUs on them all and were relieved that the Tempests hadn't replaced them. We loved Spitfires!"

Although there is no record of any further operational sorties with 485 Squadron, it seems that at least ML 407 ended her war wearing the identification letters of her first RAF squadron. The war-like phase of the life of Spitfire ML 407 was now complete. She had flown 174 operations totalling 204 hours 45 minutes with six squadrons*, all of which were nominated foreign or Commonwealth units. In fact, only four of her pilots hailed from the UK. On April 26th, no doubt as a result of all those hours of strenuous flying, ML 407 was received by 151 RU at Wevelgem, for a well-earned rest and re-fit.

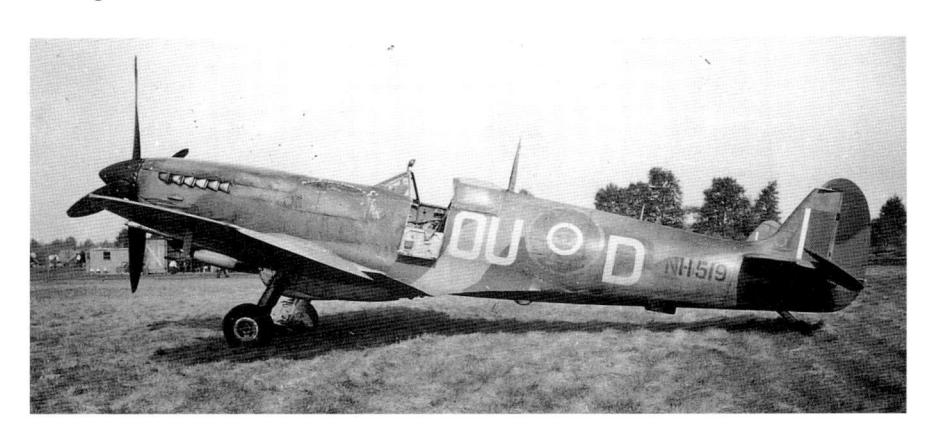

Test and Delivery Section, 151 RU(A)

85 Group, 2nd TAF at B.55 Wevelgem

The European war had less than a fortnight to run when ML 407 left 485 Squadron for the last time. She had logged just over 200 hours operational flying time in the year since she was taken on charge. Quite a respectable tally for a front line veteran. Now she was either slightly damaged or due for overhaul and inspection and for this she was flown to 151 RU (Repair Unit) at B.55 Wevelgem, near Courtrai, in Belgium. F/Lt James Pickering was Chief Test Pilot.

"After repair or modification, aircraft were passed to me and performance-tested on a similar programme to that of Castle Bromwich, but applied to all types of TAF aircraft. They were brought to operational standard and armed so they could be returned to squadrons ready in all respects (except for radio crystals then in short supply) for operational use. At least three test flights were normally required for each aircraft, though some needed many more. Details of flights were entered on 'snag sheets' after each sortie, until aircraft were fully serviceable. Successive flights of individual aircraft may not have been made by the same pilot, so there were random checks on each other's work that helped to maintain an even standard of performance acceptability. Reinforcement aircraft for 2nd TAF delivered to 151 from MUs in the UK had the same treatment, to maintain a pool of operationally serviceable aircraft.

"I was Officer Commanding Test and Delivery Flight (T & D) and as such was Chief Test Pilot. I had a team of ferry pilots in addition to four other test pilots and a variety of communication aircraft. The Group Captain was an engineering officer with 'Wings' and he sometimes flew the aircraft. I was also Senior General Duties Officer of the Unit and once had to endorse the Group Captain's Log Book for force-landing a Tempest with wheels down. A belly landing normally did less damage and was safer.

"My deputy was F/Lt Peter Fowler, who originally held a pre-war Cranwell Permanent Commission, which he had to resign after an accident (of which he remembered nothing) early in the war. Rejoining as an aircraft hand, he got onto another flying training course as a Sergeant Pilot and eventually onto a Spitfire Squadron in North Africa, from which he was re-commissioned and posted to 511 FRU as test pilot in my Flight. He was appointed to another Permanent Commission after the war and resigned from this when the Government banned supersonic flight and went to de Havilland as a test pilot.

"W/O John Grey was already a test pilot on 511 when I arrived. A sound, dependable pilot who had done operational tours on Beaufighters and Mosquitos

B.55 Wevelgem 1945. F/Lt J m Pickering orders "chocks away!" as he prepares to test-fly a Spitfire Mk IX *(Pickering)*.

mostly in daylight. He was commissioned in 1945 and stayed on 151.

"S/Ldr Anonymous was posted to me for four-engined aircraft. He had flown three tours on "heavies". His pre-war Short Service Commission was forfeit when he force-landed a Wellington at night, with a chorus-girl on board. Cashiered, he was later allowed to re-enlist in 1940 when there was a shortage of trained pilots. Very much above average as a pilot, but women were his downfall. While we were at Wevelgem, his wife in Bristol found out he had a girlfriend in Kent, and shot him (dead).

"The proper RAF Procedure for casualties was followed, and she received, whilst in jail, the usual telegram: 'We regret to inform you of the death of your husband on active service'. Mitigating circumstances reduced her sentence at the subsequent trial to one day's imprisonment.

"F/O Reg Breeze started in the RAF before the war as an apprentice fitter, but managed to re-muster to pilot. He had flown one or two tours of Spitfire operations. Like Johnny Grey he was a quiet, dependable pilot. Sadly he was the only casualty we had in my 18 months on the unit. He flew into the hill at Calais in

95

a Spitfire, trying to get through bad weather. This was quite out of character with his normal care. In marginal conditions we can all make what turns out to be an error of judgement.

"W/Cdr Richard Haine was attached to T & D Flight as supernumary test pilot for a time, pending an appointment. He had completed three tours, and was allowed no more as was current RAF practice. Such pilots were to form the nucleus of the post-war Service. Also an ex-RAF apprentice, he was a superb pilot. When he passed a Mosquito as serviceable, he would fly low across the airfield and pull straight up in a vertical climbing roll on one engine. His excuse was that if the aircraft was not safe to do this, it wasn't fit for squadron use. I never saw him do this (officially), so did not have to exert my discipline. With him, it was safe, and it was good for the morale of those who worked on the aircraft.

"Ferry pilots were all ex-operational. F/O Tommy Quirke, who after the war became a Captain with British Airways, was ex-Lockheeds (Hudsons and Venturas), mainly daylight raids on Holland. F/O Smith was shot down and had nasty burns in the Battle of Britain, but retained keenness to fly. W/O Smith was ex-Bostons. F/Sgt Clem King trained in America and came from a Typhoon squadron. F/O Ellis was an Australian, ex-Beaufighters.

"There were other ferry pilots on shorter attachment, but the above were the mainstay. After VE-Day there must have been up to a dozen ferry pilots and this

B.55 Wevelgem 1945. Test pilots P/O John Grey and F/Lt Jim Pickering (OC T & D 151 RU(A)) and ferry pilot F/Sgt Clem King *(Pickering)*.

reduced their flying. But Fowler, Grey and myself monopolised the testing to retain control of the standard.

"With the earlier ferry pilots, every opportunity was given to convert to different types of aircraft. There were however, no 'Pilot's Notes' for some aircraft, only meditation in the cockpit and unofficial advice. It is a tribute to the pilot training schemes that as long as a pilot survived the hazards of operational flying, he had few difficulties in filling a wider rôle. Ferrying was not a sinecure, as ATA statistics show. In thousands of ferry and communications flights to collect pilots, the unit broke only three aircraft. One in the Reg Breeze accident; another when I had to land a Mitchell with wheels jammed half down and an Oxford written off at Whittlesey when the pilot tried to land across the airfield into wind, instead of taking the long direction. He was supposed to pick me up after I'd delivered a Hurricane, so when we returned to Odiham by train he carried two parachutes. The only aircraft broken on test was the Tempest broken by the Group Captain CO.

"There was not an even flow of aircraft through the unit. Repairs took varying lengths of time and we maintained a pool of aircraft for immediate delivery to squadrons, together with replacements from MUs in UK. These were flown in by ATA pilots, some of whom managed to make regular deliveries to Wevelgem, because we made them welcome. The legendary Keith Jopp was one. He lost most of his left arm in the RFC (Royal Flying Corps, WWI) and had a special metal left hand that was equally useful in holding a fork, a glass or a Spitfire throttle. We suspected he only had one eye. He never made any deviation from impeccable flying discipline. Philip Wills (pre- and post-war champion glider pilot) was another, together with Garrod, Selbourne and Guest. They were keen to fly my aircraft on to the front line squadrons, but their own orders specifically forbade it, and in any case my own pilots would have revolted at the loss of flying.

"Before VE-Day, although test pilots tried to monopolise test flying, the varying flow of aircraft movements and weather factors sometimes caused waiting aircraft to accumulate. In these circumstances ferry pilots made initial tests on aircraft of their operational type. Likewise, if deliveries began to bottleneck, test pilots also flew deliveries or flew the collecting aircraft. Because of the level of competence of all the pilots, this worked without friction.

"I made no distinctions of rank on flying duties. In the crew room and in the air they were equal pilots. In the Desert Air Force after El Alamein, fighter squadrons had an officers' and pilots' combined Mess. The NCO ground crew had their own Sergeants' Mess. It was a good arrangement, but impractical for squadrons with larger crews per aircraft. On 511 and 151 we also flew and delivered four-engined types, but as with single-seat aircraft and "twins", with pilot only and no radio. It certainly kept navigation up to scratch!

"I flew more than 500 different aircraft of 28 types and marks in the 18 months I was Chief Test Pilot. It was one of the most enjoyable and interesting flying jobs ever created. However, after VE-Day the flow of aircraft was reversed, and those surplus to the shrinking TAF were returned to UK. With the tension of war over, there was a strong tendency for keenness and standards to slip. Most personnel were simply waiting for an early demobilisation.

"To maintain morale it was decided that testing standards would not be relaxed in any way. Even when it was known that aircraft would be scrapped on arrival back in the MUs, they were brought up to full operational standard before delivery. I still have harrowing memories of taking a Tempest to Lichfield and its tail being chopped off before I even had time to remove my parachute.

"My Log Book tells me that I did an engine and airframe test on Spitfire IX '407 on August 26th 1945. I'm sure the policy of maintaining the testing standard was right (even so I had seven engine failures between VE-Day and demobilisation in October, though without aircraft damage) and that this insistence ensured ML 407 was suitable for later re-issue.

"Delivery of ML 407 to High Ercall would almost certainly have been by one of the Unit's pilots. ATA had ceased to deliver to the Continent after VE-Day and ferry pilots on 151 were substantially increased because there were many surplus RAF pilots from disbanding TAF squadrons."

ML 407's Airframe Log Book recorded her final total of hours, as 319 hours and 50 minutes, on September 22nd 1945. If it is assumed that the entry was made after she was flown to 29 MU, then the ferry-flight from Belgium must have taken place on, or before, that date. On September 27th ML 407 was officially taken on charge by 29 MU High Ercall where she remained, dozing in well-maintained storage, for almost five years (having been accounted-for in the Home Census of 1946, and another census at the end of 1949). But just over six months later she was re-awakend. Another shape, another rôle and another Service awaited her.

W/O Smith, W/O King, non-flying W/O, F/Lt Pickering, F/Lt Fowler, S/Ldr Allen and F/O Quirke, Wevelgem, summer 1945 *(Pickering)*.

Flight Lieutenant James Pickering AFC, AE and bar

(Pickering).

Jim Pickering enlisted in the RAFVR in 1937 and gained his first PPL (Private Pilot's Licence) the following year. He was mobilised in August 1939 and began flying Sea Gladiators on attachment to 769(F), 759(F) and 804(F) Fleet Air Arm Squadrons. During June 1940 he flew Spitfires with 64 Squadron at Kenley, but in July embarked on the aircraft-carrier *HMS Argus* (with "Force H") as a member of 418 Flight, bound for Malta. Having flown his Hurricane from *Argus* to the island, he served with 261 Squadron on both Hurricanes and the Malta Gladiators *"Faith"*, *"Hope"* and *"Charity"*.

In April 1941 Pickering transferred to the Middle East and briefly joined 80 Squadron in Greece. Later he became involved in air deliveries on the Takoradi route from West Africa to Egypt. Further ferrying duties also took him to the American Volunteer Group (AVG) *"Flying Tigers"* in China with Warhawks. 1942 found Jim Pickering in the Western Desert Air Force with 80 Squadron (Hurricanes) and 145 Squadron (Spitfires), where he remained until '43, often flying a captured Italian three-engined Savoia-Marchetti SM 79. He admits his activities during the forgoing period included "various engagements of the kind usual for fighter pilots".

Of about 20 forced and precautionary landings the most memorable (because they were the only ones in which the aircraft was damaged) include a Hurricane engine-failure behind enemy lines and rescue by the Long Range Desert Group (LRDG), putting a Boston down on a Persian beach, and a nasty mess landing a Mitchell with wheels partially retracted.

Back in Europe, he left operational flying to go to 3501 Servicing Unit, Cranfield (testing Spitfire and Mustang modifications) and as a F/Lt was posted OC T&D 511 FRU, Odiham and 151 RU(A), Wevelgem. He was de-mobbed in October 1945 and his decorations include AFC, AE and bar, Battle of Britain Clasp and "the usual campaign medals".

In 1946 Pickering renewed his PPL which was eventually re-issued to include autogyros. He re-joined the Volunteer Reserve and remained until its demise in 1957. From '57 to '75 he continued his commitment to the Service in the RAFVR(T) and began to use his flying talents as an aviation archaeologist. By 1994 he had amassed over 6,000 hours as pilot in command (P1) on about 60 types. Total time on about 90 types is over 7,000 hours. As an aviation archaeologist he has discovered and photographed some tens-of-thousands of unknown archaeological sites in England and Europe, still with a valid PPL in 1994.

151 Repair Unit (Aircraft) 85 Group, 2nd TAF at B.55 Wevelgem, Belgium

Spitfire ML 346, OU-G, of 485 Squadron at 511 FRU, Odiham. Having been written-off it is undergoing spares recovery in the hands of Cpl Lazenby of Salvage Division. This aircraft was flown by W/O H.M. "Mick" Esdaile during June 1944 but sustained Cat.B operational damage on July 17th and was re-categorised Cat.E by 511 RSU on July 27th *(Thomas)*.

In October 1943 a new unit was formed at 13 MU Henlow. The unit was to be responsible for the recovery and repair of all types of aircraft and RAF motor transport which had suffered accident or battle damage in the forthcoming invasion of Europe. In order to keep up with the advancing forces it was to be completely mobile and would obviate the need to send damaged machines and engines back to UK for repair.

Its organisation took into account the lessons learned from the formation and work of a similar unit that went earlier with the 1st TAF to North Africa. It had a high percentage of officers, non-commissioned officers and airmen with experience of repairing and servicing aircraft in difficult conditions in the Near- and Far-East.

Initially called 511 Forward Repair Unit (FRU) it included a Salvage Division (SD), Motor Transport Overhaul and Repair Division (MRD), Airframe Repair Division (ARD), Engine Repair Division (ERD) with a Propeller

Repair Section and Test and Dispatch Section (T & D). As far as aircraft were concerned, it was primarily concerned with types used by the new 2nd Tactical Air Force, which were mainly Spitfires, Typhoons, Tempests, Mustangs, Mosquitos and Mitchells.

Soon the FRU was established at Odiham, most of the personnel living under canvas in a muddy encampment which stretched as far as the eye could see. There were separate repair sections for twin-engined aircraft and single-engined aircraft, main-planes and power-plants (sub-divided into Wright Cylone, Allison, Napier Sabre, and Rolls-Royce Merlin). It was well equipped with all the necessary workshop facilities including large industrial compressors which were used for pneumatic rivetting and drilling. The General Engineering Squadron attached to the Engine Repair Division provided welding, blacksmithing, carpentry, upholstery and general back-up facilities for ARD, ERD and MRD. To help the new unit gain experience, damaged aircraft from UK were selected and fed into Odiham.

As far as the Spitfire repair Flight was concerned there was a complement of between 120 and 150 tradesmen who dealt with a wide variety of airframe

Spitfire Mk IXc, ON-C, of 124 Squadron under repair at 511 FRU Odiham, 1944 *(Coates)*.

Spitfire Mk IX NH 483, 5R-B, of 33 Squadron with 511 FRU at Odiham, 1944 (Coates).

repairs, apart from wings which went to the main-plane section. Typical of the aircraft received were victims of wheels-up landings, heavy landings and "nose-overs" with engine and propeller damage. In this way experience was gained in changing "skins" on the fuselage (for example those from frame 12 to frame 16 which were often damaged in wheels-up landing) and dealing with damaged undercarriage brackets and tail-wheel assemblies. If the fuselage frames themselves were damaged this could mean changing from a half to a third of a frame at the bottom. In the case of a nose-over, engine bearers were checked for correct alignment, changed if necessary and the tapered attachment-bolts reamed accordingly. Sometimes wing attachment-bolt holes sustained damage when salvage crews dismounted the main-planes for transit and these needed to be reamed-out also. Another common wing repair was the replacement of wrinkled skins due to dive-bombing stress.

Many of these jobs went far beyond the normal Spitfire repair schedule and sometimes the work carried-out was not strictly to the book. For instance, when a complete frame 5 was transferred from one Spitfire fuselage to another (without the aid of any jigs) it was simply checked by basic rigging techniques after the aircraft had been re-assembled – measuring from wing tips to the tail-plane tip. The proof was that the aeroplane flew satisfactorily.

Emphasis was placed on a high degree of workmanship in the repair shops and standards were kept up to those of the Maintenance Units. All repairs were "joggled", countersunk, rivetted and "dimpled" to maintain a smooth finish of the fuselage skin over every repair. It was a remarkable achievement, particularly when many of the tradesmen were conscripts who had been turned into skilled workers by the RAF within two or three months.

The advance party of the FRU went to France about the end of July 1944 and consisted of the Salvage Division, MRD, and mobile workshops. In the event, aircraft casualties were not as high as expected during the invasion campaign and the Salvage Division and MRD went their own way. Meanwhile the main airframe and engine element didn't move to the Continent until late in the year. When the move came (at the end of November) low-loaders were used to move the equipment from Odiham, including the large compressors, to landing-craft which shipped everything to Belgium. The convoy to its new base consisted of about 1,000 vehicles.

The renamed 151 Repair Unit (Aircraft), or 151 RU(A) installed itself at the former Belgian Air Force flying training school at B.55 Wevelgem, T & D being the last to arrive later in December. The first task however, which was accomplished by an Airfield Construction Unit, was to build roads for aircraft movement. Accommodation was cold but not as wet as the tents the airmen were used-to, since they were able to occupy the shells of barracks and mess blocks which they quickly set about making livable. The Germans had made a great effort to camouflage the airfield, suspending nets from tall poles to cover some of the buildings and hangars. Some hangars were partially underground and were disguised with elaborate constructions of wood and chicken-wire representing local houses and cafés, complete with windows and doors. When dismantled they provided fuel to keep the airmen warm in the bitter weather.

ERD took over a carpet factory in the village and ARD occupied permanent hangars on the airfield, which were supplemented by four canvas Bessoneaux hangars. The Propeller Repair Section used a building on the airfield alongside the railway line, Mobile Repair Party (MRP) was based on the northern perimeter, and T & D had a large dispersal at the Bissigem end, with a Bessoneaux for respraying finished aircraft.

151 RU received damaged aircraft direct from the operational squadrons or via the Unit's own MRP "crash-gangs", which consisted of an NCO and five tradesmen in specially equipped Thorneycroft lorries, who would locate downed aircraft from map references, in any country anywhere in the British and American zones. Working from their mobile workshop their task was then to inhibit the engine, strip down the aircraft and send it back by road, or do a temporary repair so it could be flown in to Wevelgem by a ferry pilot. Other custom was provided by wounded Lancasters, Fortresses, Liberators, Bostons and Havocs which dropped in when returning from raids, though once more it transpired that the number of repairs required fell far below that which had been expected.

Six weeks after the war was over 151 RU moved to Lüneburg, an ex-Luftwaffe base in Germany. T & D remained at Wevelgem for about another eight months before following the main party to Lüneburg, as did a small holding and servicing unit mostly for the benefit of visiting aircraft. 151 RU eventually became No.1 Base & Repair Servicing Depot for the post-war 2nd TAF and was heavily engaged in services for the Berlin Air Lift in 1948.

151 RU was the largest unit of its kind ever formed by the RAF comprising, at its zenith, more than 3,000 officers and men. One of its members sums it up well. "This was brilliant planning by SHAEF (Supreme Headquarters Allied Expeditionary Force) and 2nd TAF. The concept, which had been tried and refined in the Western Desert, was brought to fruition with the setting-up of our mobile aircraft recovery and repair units and must have made no small contribution to the success of our air forces. 151 RU(A) was a self-contained but completely mobile airfield, with its own HQ administration, staff, stores, catering, motor transport, medical and dental units – quite apart from the aircraft and engineering side. Imagine the scale and extent of the logistics involved – and we were only one of many units in 2nd TAF."

Engineers Ken Hogg and J.D. Wright of 151 RU(A), T & D Flight, working on a Mustang III. Spitfire Mk XIV RM 623, MN-A, of 350 (Belgian) Squadron is beyond *(Wright)*.

Trainer Conversion of ML 407
Vickers-Armstrongs Limited, Southampton

ML 407 remodelled as a two-seat trainer by Vickers-Armstrongs, at Eastleigh before collection by the Irish Air Corps in 1951. RP (rocket projectile) equipment was specifically ordered *(Arnold)*.

First mooted in 1941, a trainer version of the Spitfire was never built in wartime Britain, because it was felt that it would divert too much effort from the production and development of vital fighter and photo-reconnaissance versions. Also the current training sequence, of de Havilland Tiger Moth to North American Harvard or Miles Master to Spitfire, had proved quite satisfactory. Interestingly, the Russian Air Force during WWII did its own local modification of standard airframes and made a successful 2-seat operational-conversion trainer. This was their Spitfire Mk IX UTI (Uchebno Trenirovochnii Istrebityel).

After the war there were plenty of surplus Spitfires Mk IXs and Vickers built a prototype two-seater as a private venture (a conversion of Mk VIII MT 818 with the civil registration G-AIDN). It was advertised as the "Spitfire High Performance Trainer" and eventually modest overseas orders were secured. No Mk VIII trainers went into production, but a Mk IX version ran to 20 aircraft and involved some major surgery to the airframe. A fully instrumented second cockpit for the

Fresh from the factory on delivery-day, Spitfire T9s 162 (ML 407) and 163 (TE 308) await acceptance by pilots from the Irish Air Corps, July 29th or 30th 1951 *(Arnott)*.

*The Vickers-Armstrongs specification document for the 2-seat trainers, refers to the Mk VIII as a "Type 499" and the Mk IX as a "Type 502".

instructor was dropped into the rear fuselage, behind and slightly higher than the student's, which in turn was repositioned some 13½ inches further forward than normal. This displacement meant a smaller fuel tank behind the engine, the reduced capacity being made-up by wing-tanks in the cannon and ammunition bays providing a total of 94 gallons. The aircraft's range without a drop-tank, including an allowance for take-off, climb to 20,000 feet and 15 minutes combat, was quoted as 234 miles and its duration of cruise, at 20,000 feet, as 1.03 hours. All the Mk IX trainers also had the broad-chord (pointed) rudder fitted.

The RAF showed little enthusiasm, but the two-seater was evaluated at A & AEE Boscombe Down in early 1947 and although handling was considered to be similar to operational single-seaters, as a "schoolroom" the cockpit layout was judged to leave something to be desired. The instructor's cockpit position made take-off and landing monitoring a little difficult, but by no means impossible.

In June 1950 Vickers-Armstrongs submitted a quote, in response to an approach by the Irish Army Air Corps, for the supply of six Mk IX trainers (designated Supermarine Type 509 *). The six Spitfires bought-back from the RAF to fulfil the order were MJ 627, MJ 772, MK 721, PV 202, ML 407 and TE 308. The RAF sold ML 407 to Vickers-Armstrongs as "Non-Effective Stock" in July 1950, and the Spitfire was moved from 29 MU High Ercall to Vickers-Armstrongs Ltd, Hursley Park Division, for conversion in October.

The cost was quoted as £12,250 ex-works and equipment was to include RP (rocket projectile) gear, no armament, recording camera, turret-sight in the rear cockpit, and a 50-gallon "torpedo" overload fuel tank. The contract was signed on September 21st 1950, the terms of payment being cash on acceptance of each aircraft at the works of Messrs Vickers-Armstrongs.

By the summer of 1951 the batch of trainers for the Irish Army Air Corps was nearing completion, deliveries taking place between May and July. The six Spitfire T9s were painted by Vickers-Armstrongs to the specifications supplied by the IAAC and eventually numbered 158-163. By July 16th ML 407 was already being referred to on documentation as "162".

It seems likely, from the Ministry of Civil Aviation Log Book of ML 407, that she had been already re-engined once, perhaps by 151 RU or 29 MU, with Merlin 66 194013/A.488844. Nevertheless Vickers-Armstrongs installed 186327/A.483001, which was ground-run for 25 minutes on July 18th. Spitfire 162 also received a new Rotol propeller.

Vickers were allowed by the Registration Board to use their own markings when test-flying aircraft which were being prepared for sale to foreign Governments, provided such flights were confined to their own aerodromes. Therefore, for her initial 30-minute test flight at Eastleigh Airport on July 24th and for two further 20-minute sorties next day, ML 407 was allocated the Vickers' number G.15-175.

Irish Air Corps
Flying Training Schools, Baldonnel

"B" Flight, Baldonnel 1952. Seated left to right, Lt Kirwan, Capt Healy, Lt O'Keefe, and B. O'Reilly *(Healy)*.

The two-seat Spitfires were collected from Eastleigh and flown to Baldonnel in pairs, 158 and 159 on June 5th, 160 and 161 on June 29th and 162 and 163 on July 30th. For its 20-minute acceptance-flight and subsequent ferry-flight the pilot of 162 was Captain H. F. Howard and Captain Healy flew 163. When taken on charge by the Air Corps Flying Schools, 162 had logged over 320 hours of airframe time, more than 200 of them on wartime operations.

"We were flown to Eastleigh by Lt Coughlan in an old Anson (141) on July 29th," recalls Capt Howard. "There we were met by the Vickers people, a Mr Rasmussen was in charge. He arranged hotel accommodation and entertained us handsomely. We handed over the cash before they let us near the Spitfires, and then I did a flight around Eastleigh circuit to check the aircraft. It was a grass aerodrome and there wasn't much runway to spare for take-off and landing.

162 receives the annual blessing from the Padre "Father Bill" O'Reardon at Baldonnel. Captain Tim Healy, Flight Commander of all six Spitfires in the Training School, is the cap-less officer *(Kearns)*.

"We flew VFR (Visual Flight Rules) at about 2,000 feet direct from Eastleigh to Liverpool (Speke). The two aircraft were in loose formation, loose enough for a Tiger Moth to pass between us near Birmingham Tim (Healy) was leading and navigating and I was keeping station, but I did see other aircraft out of the corner of my eye, including the Tiger Moth.

We re-fuelled at Speke and continued along the north coast of Wales, via Rhyl, Great Ormes Head, and Holyhead to Baldonnel. When we arrived we could see that everybody had come out to welcome us, so we gave an aerobatic display before landing."

162 in a publicity photograph with a couple of ancient bombs which she certainly never carried in the Air Corps. Neither is there any sign of RP hard-point pylons *(Healy)*.

However for Capt Healy in 163, this turned out to be a rather embarrassing arrival. Because of the wind conditions at Baldonnel it was necessary to land on a rather short strip, approached directly over the Officers' Mess. The aircraft's undercarriage failed to lock down, and the brand new Spitfire slid to a less-than-ceremonious halt on its belly. Luckily it was at that time still a grass airfield, so there was little damage and 163 was soon back in the air again. But so far as Tim Healy was concerned, nothing could mitigate "the appalling indignity of bending a new aircraft on delivery."

After the accident the undercarriage indicator lights in the cockpit were modified to provide greater visibility, and the linkage between the front and rear cockpit undercarriage operating levers altered to give more positive locking for the pupil.

By March 1960, 162 had lost her RP pylons *(Skillen)*.

Despite this inauspicious incident Healy, as Flight Commander in charge of all six, went on to form a good working relationship with the new Spitfire trainers. As someone with many years of experience, using them in the rôle to which it was adapted, his opinion contrasts with that of the RAF. He endorses the aircraft as a "suitable advanced trainer for its time" and disagrees with the jaundiced A & AEE evaluation except on two points. The first reflects the personal experience related above.

"The Spitfire T9 was always flown solo from the front cockpit, but the master control box which gave a very positive indication of undercarriage hydraulic operation sequence, was in the rear cockpit. The front seat undercarriage lever was a very short one, with very limited travel – the last fraction of an inch movement

162 in use as an instructional airframe at Baldonnel in 1960 *(Waring)*.

Captain Henry Howard, Irish Air Corps

Young Henry Howard was at Castleknock College between 1935 and '38. From there he could see the aircraft from nearby Baldonnel aerodrome flying overhead. He decided that was the life for him, so between the age of 17 and 18 he applied to join both the RAF and the Irish Air Corps. He was successful on both counts, but was called to the Air Corps first.

His first ever flight was in a Miles Magister in May 1940, when he started training with the Irish Air Corps. He went on to fly Avro Cadets, Avro 626s, Hawker Hinds and Hectors, Gloster Gladiators, Westland Lysanders, Miles Masters, Hurricanes, Seafires, Spitfires, Fairey Battle, de Havilland Chipmunks and Doves and Percival Provosts. Apart from flying duties his service included Flight Administration and Survey Photography (both oblique and vertical). He went on to complete the Staff Course including tactical operations.

On retirement from the Air Corps in 1956, he joined Aer Lingus, spending the rest of his career on DC-3s, Viscounts, Boeing 707s and 737s.

(Howard).

Captain Tim Healy, Irish Air Corps

Tim Healy originally joined the Army as a (TA) volunteer in the summer of 1939. In September he was called up for permanent service and he joined the Air Corps in May 1940 as a Cadet, for a Short Service Commission. His first flight in a Miles Magister was on June 6th, and training continued on Avro Cadet and Hawker Hector. Having completed his "Wings" course in October 1941, he went straight onto a Flying Instructor's course, on completion of which he spent a year with the Fighter Squadron on Gloster Gladiators.

From 1943-67 he was engaged in the training rôle as a Qualified Flying Instructor (QFI) at the Training Schools, Baldonnel. He was promoted to Captain Flight Commander in 1948, before attending Central Flying School (RAF), Little Rissington for a year. In 1957 he became Commandant of the Schools, and 10 years later, as a Lieutenant-Colonel, was the Station Commander at Gormanston. In 1972, now Wing Commander Flying, he was back at Baldonnel to become Station Commander in 1976, two years before retirement.

In 5,468 hours of flying (575 on Spitfires) he sampled 45 types the latest being Fouga Magister and C.130. Interesting experiences include writing off a Hawker Hector in 1941 while illegally low-flying, and a Lysander in 1942, when after loss of power in cloud he "descended at a prodigious rate of

(Healy).

knots, to break cloud overhead a strip known as "the Guinness Airfield". He managed to get into the field alright, but getting through the trees cost his Lysander its wings. "The fuselage was OK." In 1953 he was forced to ditch an Anson in the river Shannon when an engine failed on a routine flight.

Tim Healy's Log Book records 61 hours flown in Spitfire 162, between August 1951 and July 1960.

being the one which locked down the legs. Secondly, some instruments were difficult to see in the back, particularly the RPM indicator. The trainers were used for air-to-ground gunnery and were very satisfactory in the rôle, with their Browning .303-inch machine guns (rockets and bombs were not used). Perhaps the worst trouble was the tendency of the coolant to boil over after the inevitable slow taxying by pupils."

When the Spitfire trainers arrived in 1951, the Fighter Squadron at Gormanston was equipped with Seafire LF Mk IIIs. But during the early '50s the number of Seafires diminished rapidly with little or no hope of replacements. So it was that the Spitfires were taken over periodically by the Fighter Squadron, for continuation training. 162 twice transferred in this way during her service in Eire.

By the end of November 1956, when her engine was removed at the start of a 400-hour check, the aeroplane had added 363 hours 15 minutes to her airframe total. It was replaced by another Merlin 66, number 308113, on March 1st next year. 162 logged a further 399 hours 20 minutes before her last flight with the Irish Air Corps, which was on July 8th 1960. Once more due for a 400-hour check, at this point ML 407 was grounded and relegated to serve as an instructional airframe, at Baldonnel, until offered for sale in 1968.

162 at Baldonnel, April 11th 1960 *(Waring)*.

Probably the last formation flight of the four remaining airworthy IAC Spitfire T9s, 1960. Interestingly, the aircraft represent four different generations of colour-scheme *(Ferguson via Waring and MacCarron).*

Spitfire in Limbo
Cricklewood and Strathallan

On March 4th 1968, Mr. N. A. W. (Tony) Samuelson of Samuelson Films, Cricklewood, bought several of the remaining Irish two-seat Spitfires to use as back-up airframes for the forthcoming production of the film "Battle of Britain" and 162, the former ML 407, was one of them. In the event the aircraft was never even re-assembled, let alone filmed.

Two years later Sir William Roberts bought the sad remains of ML 407 in April and moved the fuselage and wings to Flimwell. In March 1972 the dismembered aircraft moved north to the home of his Strathallan Collection near Auchterarder, Perthshire. Over the next few years some desultory preservation work was carried out, but it was not until August 1979, when Businessman and Engineer Nick Grace bought all the remaining Spitfire spares on behalf of Island Trading Limited (which included the stripped airframe of ML 407) that her restoration to airworthiness was assured. On October 29th 1979, ML 407 began the long haul down to St Merryn, the old Fleet Air Arm base in Cornwall. She was registered to Island Trading by the Civil Aviation Authority on February 1st 1980, with letters appropriate to her Mark – G-LFIX.

Nick Grace had determined to rebuild the aeroplane "purely to be able to fly it" – a task which would take four and a half years of painstaking work spread over a six-year period, virtually all of which he was to accomplish himself.

"I took it on because I've always said that I wanted to fly a Spitfire, and there was no way that anyone was going to let me fly a Spitfire. They weren't going to say to me 'There's my Spitfire over there old chap. Off you go and do what you want to do and, you know, please bring it back in one bit'!"

ML 407 languishing in store at Shoreham in 1971 (Arnold).

Restoration
St Merryn Airfield

Unloading at St Merryn, October 29th 1979. Nick Grace is nearest the van *(Grace)*.

The aircraft arrived at St Merryn in component form, packed into two Pickfords' lorries. The main airframe – wings, fuselage and tail sections – had been stripped of internal fittings and all the smaller parts were in tea chests. The larger parts were packed individually, and among these were two zero-time Merlin 25 engines and one zero-time propeller.

The first job was to sort out what was missing, with the help of Dick Melton, ex-Chief Engineer of the Battle of Britain Memorial Flight and long-time personal friend. It was anticipated that after a clean, repair as required and re-protection, the overhauled parts would be ready for reassembly. Unfortunately the airframe was found to be rivetted with magnesium alloy rivets (green and marked with an "X") and that meant eventually internal electrolytic corrosion would cause the heads to fall off! The fuselage would have to be disassembled and rebuilt with new rivets and damaged skins (about 30%) replaced. This process was repeated on all the main structures.

In addition to the restoration work, a major modification of the wings was planned, to increase the fuel capacity from 25 gallons to 60 gallons per wing, which would give a total capacity (including fuselage tank) of 159 gallons. This modification was completed with the help of Frank Robertson, ex-Chief Preliminary Designer of Vought in America, and Jim Tucker of the CAA Design Office at Redhill, who assisted considerably throughout the project. Another

Two-speed single-stage Merlin 25, used in a lighter ML 407 compares well from 0-3,000 feet with heavier 66, plus full warload *(Grace)*.

ML 407 (162) and PV 202 (161) and parts at St Merryn *(Grace)*.

Port wing stripped for inspection and restoration *(Grace)*.

Re-skinning the fuselage *(Grace)*.

Standard canopy placed on rear cockpit when planning new "custom" enclosure (Grace).

Airframe re-assembled, engine installation almost completed, Christmas 1984 (Grace).

radical Grace design concept was the stream-lined rear cockpit canopy and glazed "tunnel" linking it to the forward hood (since adopted for the restoration of two-seaters PV 202 and PT 462), which replaced the clumsy-looking Vickers arrangement.

To overcome delays caused by missing parts and other problems, the refitting of the fuselage was started before the completion of the wings (which were worked on concurrently). The fuselage, including all systems, was completed on July 10th, 1984, and the wings were re-married to it over Christmas. On January 6th 1985, ML 407 was ready for engine runs.

"It didn't actually get going first time," admitted Nick, "which was a slight embarrassment to say the least. Not because of a fault but because of what's known as 'finger trouble', it kept endeavouring to go but the darned thing wouldn't actually run. Then all-of-a-sudden 'the coin dropped', we hadn't turned the switches on in the rear cockpit! We felt like a couple of bunnies really – turned the switches on in the back cockpit – then the blades hardly went round a turn before it was running."

Starting a Merlin engine and doing a power run can be overwhelming for those who have never experienced it – the noise, smell and most of all, the way the engine can throw around an aircraft weighing 7,330 pounds. At times the mainwheels are nine inches to a foot off the ground, despite the aircraft being tied down at the tail.

With engine ground-running successfully accomplished, the Spitfire was declared complete and ready, with Permit to Test issued by Mr G. Rigby of Bristol

Dick Melton running-up the Merlin, St Merryn, April 15th 1985 *(Arnold)*.

CAA Office on April 10th 1985. Bad weather delayed the first flight, which was finally made by Nick Grace on April 16th.

"First Flight"

After start-up and ground checks Nick taxied the aircraft out and first made a high-speed ground run, to identify ground-handling characteristics. The only unknown quantity remaining was aileron-trim which, Nick knew, always had to be established by test-flying a Spitfire.

"Back-track and I make a quick final check, as by now temperatures are increasing fast. I line-up and apply zero boost, approximately 900 hp. Things start happening fast and in no time 50 knots is indicated. Although there is a tendency to swing, this is easily overcome by rudder. At 55 knots a quick lift off the ground to establish the aileron trim – almost neutral – then back on the ground for more speed. At 80 knots – airborne without help. What a moment! Retract the gear immediately to keep temperature down,* increase to plus 8 boost, speed up to 155 knots and climbing at 2,000 feet a minute – what a fabulous experience. What an unbelievable aircraft – flying as though it had never done anything else. All manoeuvres are easy and naturally balanced.

"Up to 5,000 feet to test the stall, gear and flaps down, throttle closed. Speed coming back and back and back – 80 knots, 70 knots, 60 knots, 50 knots – still no stall, but very sloppy at 50 knots. Decide that is slow enough. Back for a landing.

"Approach at 70 knots, forward visibility is not as bad as expected, drift in over the fence and flare. She drops on in a beautiful three-point landing and stops without trouble in about 550 yards."

* The Spitfire's undercarriage masks the underwing coolant radiators in the "down" position.

G-LFIX makes her first flight from St Merryn on April 15th 1985 *(Grace)*.

ML 407 by *"FlyPast"* photographer Duncan Cubitt, January 1986 *("FlyPast")*.

Actually Nick had to "over-shoot" on the first attempt to land, because the crowd of friends and local well-wishers who had turned-up to witness the event spilled all over the runway, and mis-interpreted his gestures from the cockpit as appreciative waves. "They obviously couldn't hear what I was shouting." But once safely down, it was time for a traditional "champagne-shower" celebration for the *two* delighted occupants of the Spitfire, for Nick had insisted that his wife, Carolyn, be in the rear seat. "It was a wonderful shared moment" she later revealed.

The full test-flight programme was completed by Viv Bellamy, from Land's End (St Just) airfield. This WWII combat pilot and one-time Spitfire owner conceded, "I did anticipate the odd problem, but far from it, it was a beautiful aeroplane." After years of waiting and being slowly stripped of everything, ML 407 has returned to her true element.

Flying Colours

With the engineering successfully concluded, Nick Grace turned his attention to the matter of painting of ML 407. He decided to repaint the Spitfire as she had appeared three days before D-Day, as OU-V of 485 Squadron. The author had made contact with Johnnie Houlton in January 1983 and he had turned up several

Ron White and Vic Strange meet again with ML 407 at the Spitfire Society's 50th Anniversary of the prototype's first flight at Eastleigh, on March 5th 1986 *(Smallwood)*.

Nick Grace, Johnnie Houlton and Gaby Seydel with ML 407 at St Just Aerodrome on July 22nd 1985 *(TVS)*.

photographs of ML 407 among his friends in New Zealand, which provided an invaluable source of reference. These enabled Nick Grace to create an accurate reconstruction of the wartime look of the aircraft. He made every effort to reproduce the original MAP (Ministry of Aircraft Production) camouflage and national insignia colours, official disruptive patterns on the upper surfaces and the dimensions and positioning of the markings.

Reunion

When the independent television company TVS planned a documentary in which ML 407 was to figure largely,* a nostalgic reunion was inevitable with some of the characters from her past. Filming began at St Just Aerodrome at Land's End on July 22nd 1985 and it was there that Johnnie Houlton, Jackie Moggridge and Gaby Seydel were re-united with ML 407.

For Johnnie the time in between just fell away when he sat once more in the familiar cockpit of OU-V, 41 years after that last sortie over the Normandy battlefield. In hazy sunshine Spitfire ML 407 lifted both her first RAF pilot and her latest and most intimate owner effortlessly up into the English sky and out over the Channel, which Johnnie Houlton had crossed so many times taking battle to the enemy in "Fortress Europe".

* *"The Perfect Lady"* TVS 1985.

Nick and Carolyn Grace

Nick Grace adjusts his wife's parachute before their first flight together in ML 407, April 16th 1985 *(Grace)*.

ML 407 rolled-out for the first engine run, St Merryn, January 6th 1985 *(Jeremy Flack)*.

Nick Grace, Gaby Seydel and Johnnie Houlton with ML 407, St Just Aerodrome, July 22nd 1985 *(TVS)*.

1986 was a big year for Spitfires because it was the 50th anniversary of the prototype's first flight and the Spitfire Society invited Nick and his aeroplane to their private function at Eastleigh. On the day, perhaps with another touch of "stage-fright" which echoed Johnnie Houlton's mishap on D-Day 1944, she again lost the tips of her propeller blades (and sustained slight damage to the cowlings and radiator housings), this time in an unscheduled wheels-up arrival. ML 407's veteran ground crew Vic Strange and Ron White, who last saw their charge in 1944, lost no time in consoling a rueful Nick with stories of "proper prangs" and judged accurately that the damage was slight. Another guest on this occasion was one time 485 Squadron "B" Flight Commander W/Cdr Owen Hardy (retired), under the authority of whom both the Spitfire and the two Flight Mechanics had operated. He had even flown ML 407 a couple of times himself. Hardy lived less than a mile from the Graces on Selsey Bill, where ML 407 had joined 485 (NZ) Squadron at 135 Airfield in April 1944. However 42 years later, the Spitfire was hangared at Goodwood airfield (known as Westhampnett during the war) – which had itself been home to 485 Squadron in the Spring of 1943. Owen Hardy told Nick of his delight at hearing the familiar Merlin's "call" low overhead, and later his even greater pleasure when he saw a Spitfire which carried the identification letters of his old Squadron.

Nick Grace on a photographic sortie near Duxford, Cambridgeshire, 1987 and (inset) with Johnnie Houlton and ML 407, St Just Aerodrome, July 22nd 1985 *(Oaten and TVS)*.

As he predicted, Nick had the aircraft back in the air within three weeks, and he was full of praise for Dowty-Rotol for their unstinting help. The summer progressed with a growing number of anniversary airshows, culminating at Middle Wallop when eight Spitfires, including ML 407, flew in formation as the finale.

During 1987 and '88 Nick became much more widely known in what had become known as "The Warbird Scene". Respect for him as engineer, restorer and display-pilot grew rapidly within the fraternity. Partly as a result of *"The Perfect Lady"* and modest appearances with Jimmy Saville and Cilla Black on TV, he was

Bob Cole, CAA test-pilot of light aircraft, Gatwick, one of ML 407's most experienced pilots also played an important part in Carolyn's development with the flying of the Spitfire *(Smallwood)*.

ML 407 near Selsey, Peter Kynsey in the front and Carolyn Grace in the rear cockpit, 1989 *(Oaten)*.

Paul Bonhomme, aerobatic pilot. The most recent of ML 407's pilots *(Smallwood)*.

also adopted by a much wider public to whom he represented a "can-do" ethic which many believed to be extinct in bureaucratic Britain. With his personal charm and frank, infectious enthusiasm he always had time to respond to the most diffident approach, could explain complex flying matters simply but without talking down to the in-expert and was one of the first owners to allow non-fliers not only touch but also, on occasion, to sit in his aircraft. Anyone who had the courage to ask him a question, from toddler to pensioner merited his full and undivided attention. Nick, his Spitfire, wife Carolyn and even their two children soon inspired a unique and affectionate following. Nick took the Spitfire far and wide, visiting the Republic of Ireland, Scotland, France, Belgium, Germany and Sweden, amassing 235 hours in 48 months.

But one evening in October 1988, shortly after the completion of sequences for the TV drama *"Piece of Cake"* flying his Spanish-built "Messerschmitt 109", Hispano HA-1109 G-BOML, Nick Grace died in a car accident when returning home from a day spent working on his aircraft. Despite her loss, Carolyn never contemplated

Nick Grace and the RAF's display team, the Red Arrows, May 1988 *(Oaten)*.

disposal of the Spitfire and much later, in an interview with *"FlyPast"* magazine, she explained "The aeroplane had become part of our blood-line... it encapsulates the very essence of what I lost."

The Spitfire had always been regarded by Nick and Carolyn as a family achievement, and now more than ever it became a symbol of continuity. In *"The Perfect Lady"* Nick had said "I have put a piece of this country's heritage back in operation. It's been around since April 1944, it's survived 174 operational sorties, apparently with hardly any damage of any description. It's had a fairly graced life if you like, and I hope that it will keep it up. Certainly it will outlast me – if luck is on its side – and another few generations after that."

Now Carolyn decided that she must take up the gauntlet. "I wanted to fulfil Nick's and my ambition for me to fly solo in OU-V and certainly by the early summer of 1989 I felt it was clear that there needed to be another Grace in that cockpit".

Already she had hours of "tail-dragger" experience in her favour, having learned to fly on a Chipmunk in 1976 and she still owned her Stampe SV-4C, G-AXNW. In addition, one of her staunchest allies throughout the year following Nick's death was Peter Kynsey, whom Nick had dubbed "The finest pair of hands on the aircraft". Peter, a professional Britannia Airways pilot and first-class aerobatic pilot, was one of the very few Nick entrusted with ML 407. Perhaps the most polished and lyrical pilot of elderly fighter aircraft since the legendary Neil

Peter Kynsey, Britannia Airways and aerobatic pilot and also ML 407's chief pilot *(Kynsey)*.

Peter Kynsey and Carolyn Grace, White Waltham, July 17th 1990 *(Smallwood)*.

Carolyn Grace running-up prior to her first solo take-off *(Smallwood)*.

Carolyn's first solo take-off *(Smallwood)*.

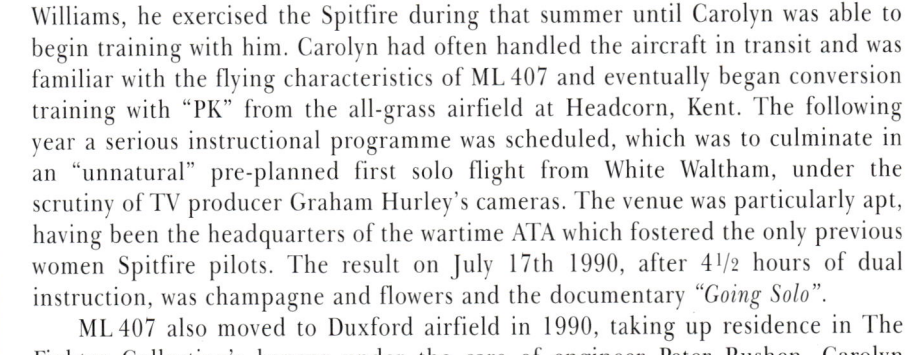

Carolyn Grace, 1993 *(March)*.

Williams, he exercised the Spitfire during that summer until Carolyn was able to begin training with him. Carolyn had often handled the aircraft in transit and was familiar with the flying characteristics of ML 407 and eventually began conversion training with "PK" from the all-grass airfield at Headcorn, Kent. The following year a serious instructional programme was scheduled, which was to culminate in an "unnatural" pre-planned first solo flight from White Waltham, under the scrutiny of TV producer Graham Hurley's cameras. The venue was particularly apt, having been the headquarters of the wartime ATA which fostered the only previous women Spitfire pilots. The result on July 17th 1990, after 4½ hours of dual instruction, was champagne and flowers and the documentary *"Going Solo"*.

ML 407 also moved to Duxford airfield in 1990, taking up residence in The Fighter Collection's hangar under the care of engineer Peter Rushen. Carolyn became a minor celebrity as the first woman to solo on a Spitfire since the 1940s, and also the first Spitfire owner/pilot of her sex. It was a natural progression to consider displaying her aeroplane herself and Peter Kynsey quietly and confidently endorsed her enterprise. In 1991 her display debut was made appropriately at White Waltham, at the "Women in Aviation" celebration. This added a new dimension to the Spitfire's public persona and generated an increased demand by the airshow organisers. Close links also continued to be reforged with the aircraft's wartime friends, many of whom have visited and become "friends of the family". Continuing a tradition begun by Nick, Carolyn has flown a number of veterans from the Spitfire's past, a privilege made incredibly possible for them by virtue of the aircraft's second seat.

In ML 407's 50th anniversary year, she was repainted with "half invasion stripes" *(Dibbs)*.

In some ways the most unique of ML 407's passengers were its wartime Flight Mechanics, Vic Strange and Ron White. Probably no ground-crew have flown aboard "their own" Spitfire ever before! On August 29th 1989, Carolyn was able to fulfil Nick's promise. "It was something Nick very much wanted" she explained to them, "to take you both for a fly. Sadly Nick didn't manage to get you in the air. But I got you there!" Their tour with Peter Kynsey took them from Goodwood airport, out over Selsey Bill, and back via Tangmere, Funtington and Merston – all airfields at which they had served. "Just like sitting on a bird" declared Vic. "A lovely sensation, especially when she banks" agreed Ron.

For ML 407's 50th birthday in 1994 a repaint was necessary. Nick's original finish was showing signs of wear-and-tear which, though many believed it gave the aircraft an authentic ambience, would ultimately have led to deterioration of the airframe if ignored. Also June would be the anniversary of D-Day, so Carolyn decided to re-apply the black and white "invasion stripes" appropriate to much of the Spitfire's operational tour of duty. Stripping off the old paint-work revealed negligible corrosion (yet another testament to Nick's thoroughness) and the new paint was applied in January, at Duxford. Carolyn was most impressed by the service she received from the Morelli Group who supplied and matched the paint meticulously to original colour specifications. Another minor "cosmetic" change occurred at this time when the logo of Carolyn's honoured sponsors Leslie and Godwin, which had been emblazoned on the Spitfire's fuel-tank cover in the traditional manner of wartime "presentation" aircraft since 1986, followed the development of the company itself and became "Leslie Nicholson".

Six years after losing Nick, ML 407 may still represent for Carolyn "the purpose for going on – for striving to do what you do" but the Spitfire has worked its magic on her, as it has on all its pilots, and always gives her and anyone who sees her fly it, an incomparable thrill.

Carolyn Grace displays the new paint-scheme near Duxford, March 1994 *(Dibbs)*.

Flying colours 1944-1985

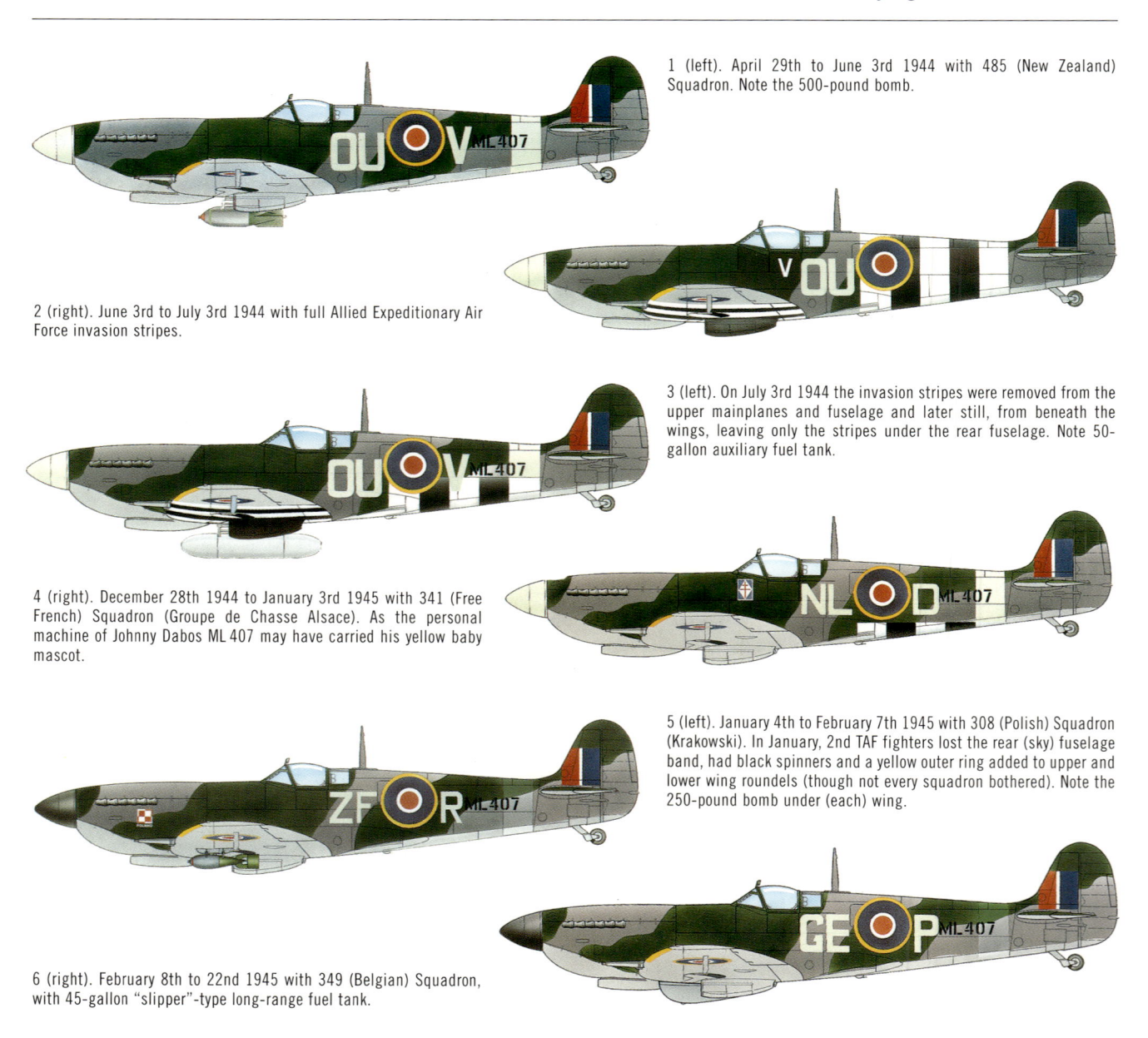

1 (left). April 29th to June 3rd 1944 with 485 (New Zealand) Squadron. Note the 500-pound bomb.

2 (right). June 3rd to July 3rd 1944 with full Allied Expeditionary Air Force invasion stripes.

3 (left). On July 3rd 1944 the invasion stripes were removed from the upper mainplanes and fuselage and later still, from beneath the wings, leaving only the stripes under the rear fuselage. Note 50-gallon auxiliary fuel tank.

4 (right). December 28th 1944 to January 3rd 1945 with 341 (Free French) Squadron (Groupe de Chasse Alsace). As the personal machine of Johnny Dabos ML 407 may have carried his yellow baby mascot.

5 (left). January 4th to February 7th 1945 with 308 (Polish) Squadron (Krakowski). In January, 2nd TAF fighters lost the rear (sky) fuselage band, had black spinners and a yellow outer ring added to upper and lower wing roundels (though not every squadron bothered). Note the 250-pound bomb under (each) wing.

6 (right). February 8th to 22nd 1945 with 349 (Belgian) Squadron, with 45-gallon "slipper"-type long-range fuel tank.

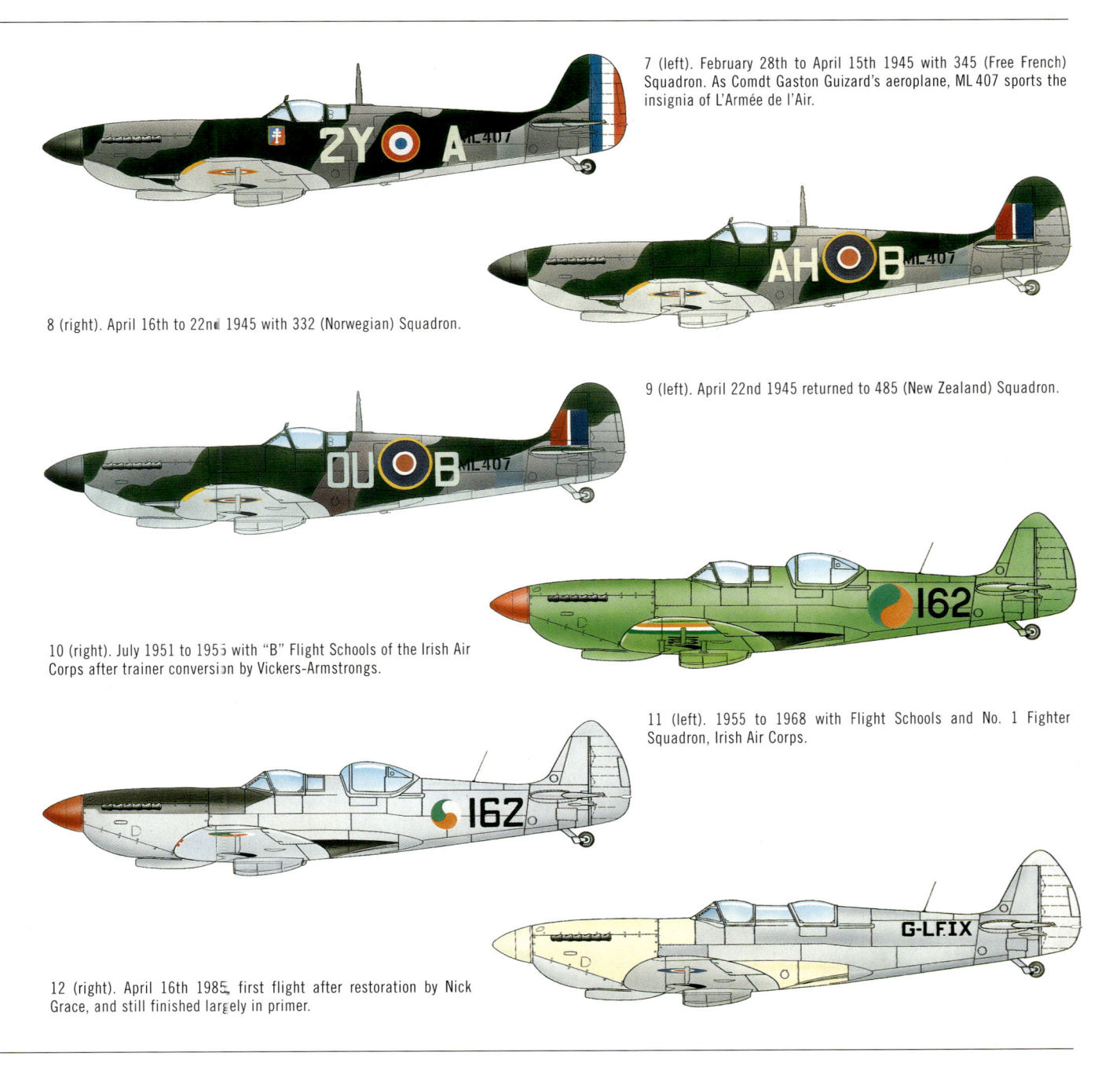

7 (left). February 28th to April 15th 1945 with 345 (Free French) Squadron. As Comdt Gaston Guizard's aeroplane, ML 407 sports the insignia of L'Armée de l'Air.

8 (right). April 16th to 22nd 1945 with 332 (Norwegian) Squadron.

9 (left). April 22nd 1945 returned to 485 (New Zealand) Squadron.

10 (right). July 1951 to 1955 with "B" Flight Schools of the Irish Air Corps after trainer conversion by Vickers-Armstrongs.

11 (left). 1955 to 1968 with Flight Schools and No. 1 Fighter Squadron, Irish Air Corps.

12 (right). April 16th 1985, first flight after restoration by Nick Grace, and still finished largely in primer.

Appendix 1: Documents

Jackie Sorour	Log Book entry April 29th 1944	132-133
RAF Form 78 (Movement Card)		134
485 Squadron	ORB Summary June 2nd-10th 1944	135
Johnnie Houlton	Log Book entry June 6th, 8th, 12th 1944	136-137
Johnnie Houlton	Log Book entry June 29th 1944	138-139
Johnnie Houlton	Combat Report June 8th 1944	140

RECORD OF

Date. 1944	Aircraft. Type.	Markings.	Engines. Type.	H.P.	Journey. From.	To.
						Brought forward
27.4.44	Beaufighter	T3105	Merlin		Cosford	Gosport
"	Oxford	NM751			Portsmouth	Little Risi...
"	Typhoon	PM561			Eastleigh	Cosford
28.4.44	Anson	MK448			Hawarden-Lyneham-Hendon
"	Spitfire	JG661			Chattis Hill	Hawarden
29.4.44	Oxford	R6350			Portsmouth	White Waltham
"	Spitfire	ML407			Lyneham	48 Sq. Selsey
"	Spit XIV	NH692	Griffon		Eastleigh	Lyneham
						Carried forward

Johnnie Houlton		Combat Report June 12th 1944			141
Johnnie Houlton		Combat Report June 29th 1944			142
349 Squadron		ORB typical daily entries February 9th-13th 1945			143
Ministry of Civil Aviation Airframe Log Book					144
Henry Howard		Log Book entry July 30th 1951			145
Nick Grace		First post-restoration flight Log Book entry April 16th 1985			146-147
Carolyn Grace		First solo flight Log Book entry July 17th 1990			146-147

FLIGHTS.   SOLO

Time of Departure.		Time of Arrival.		Time in Air.		Pilot. See Instructions (5) & (6) on flyleaf of this book.	Remarks.
Hrs.	Mins.	Hrs.	Mins.	Hrs.	Mins.		
	...	...	...	1132	30		
					45		
					40		
					30		
				02	00		
					55		
					30		
					40		
					20		
	...	...	...	138	50		

Type of Aircraft	Mark	R.A.F. Number
SPITFIRE	LF IX	M.L. 404

Contractor	Contract No.	Engine installed:—
V.A. C.B.	B981684 39	MERLIN 66. Maker's airframe No.:—

Unit or Cat'y/Cause	Station or Contractor	Date	Authority	41 or 43 Gp. Allot.
	33. M.U	23.4.44	130/25.4	50094
	485. SQD	30.4.44		124
	CATAC FB	7.10.44	435	
	R CAT A	19.10.44	49	
	470 RSJ	30.11.44	7	
	485 Sq	7.12.44	T23	
	145 Wg	28.12.44	T 182	
	341 Sq	4.1.45	T 21	
	131 Wg	4.45	T 137	
	308 Sq	11.4.45	T 99	
	349 Sq	8.2.45	T 66	
485 Sq	to 145 Wg	28.2.45	T 11	
A.M. Form 78	345 Sq	22.3.45	T 17	

Type of Aircraft	Mark	R.A.F. Number
SPITFIRE	LF IX	ML 404

Unit or Cat'y/Cause	Station or Contractor	Date	Authority	41 or 43 Gp. Allot.
	332 Sq	19.4.45	T 50	
485 Sq	to 151 RU	26.4.45	T 32	
	29 MU	27.4.45	41	
HOME CENSUS MARCH 1946.				
Census 29.12.49				
19.7.50	Sold to Vickers Armstrong as NE. aircraft	31.7.50	413/S102	106026

(*13988—10601) Wt. 48280—3679 30M 1/44 T.S. 700

(Courtesy of RAF Museum)

R.A.F. Form 540

OPERATIONS RECORD BOOK

of (Unit or Formation) 485 (NZ) SQUADRON

Page No. ONE.

No. of pages used for day ___

SECRET.

Place	Date	Time	Summary of Events	References to Appendices
A.L.G. SELSEY.	2.6.44.	15.30.	RAMROD.959. The Squadron bombed the Radar Station at Caen/Douvres La Deliverade. Instantaneous bombing. Five bombs landed round one Wuerzburg, two fell short.	
	2.6.44.	15.30.	RAMROD.959. Cover to own Spitfires bombing Radar Station at Caen/Douvres La Deliverade. Uneventful.	
	3.6.44.	18.10.	WEATHER RECCO. One Section flew a Weather Recco in the Cherbourg area. Moderate-heavy flak was encountered.	
	6.6.44.	05.35.	BEACH PATROL. This uneventful patrol was the first to be flown by the Squadron and Wing in support of operation "Overlord", and consisted of low cover to Neptune.	
	6.6.44.	10.35.	BEACH PATROL. Low cover Neptune, quite uneventful.	
	6.6.44.	14.45.	BEACH PATROL. The Squadron provided low cover to Neptune in the East Sector. Three JU 88's were seen by Blue Section led by Flying Officer J.A.Houlton, and were hotly engaged. Flying Officer Houlton destroyed one of these enemy aircraft and the section comprising of F/O.J.A.Houlton, F/Lt.K.J.Macdonald, F/O.M.C.Mayston, and F/Sgt.Atkins.K.G. shared in the destruction of a second. It is believed but as yet not confirmed that the aircraft destroyed by F/O.Houlton was the first enemy aircraft to be destroyed in combat in the Second Front.	
	6.6.44.	18.50.	BEACH PATROL. Low cover provided to Neptune. Uneventful.	
	7.6.44.	05.40.	BEACH PATROL. The Squadron provided low cover to Neptune, East Sector. 7 FW 190's and 3 JU 88's were reported to be bombing the beaches but these enemy aircraft were not encountered by the Squadron.	
	7.6.44.	10.35.	BEACH PATROL. Low cover was provided for Neptune East Sector. Flak which was accurate was encountered in the neighbourhood of Caen. Damage was sustained by two aircraft. What is believed to have been a Bofors shell severely damaged the starboard wing of the aircraft flown by F/Lt.L.S.Black, and the wireless on the aircraft flown by F/Sgt.Strahan.W.T.H. was rendered u/s after having been hit by .303.	
	7.6.44.	14.45.	BEACH PATROL. Low cover Neptune east area. Uneventful.	
	7.6.44.	19.00.	BEACH PATROL. Low cover Neptune, East area. Again uneventful.	
	8.6.44.	05.40.	BEACH PATROL. Low cover Neptune. 18 + enemy Fighter Bombers engaged. One FW 190 was destroyed by F/O.J.F.Yeatman and F/Sgt.Eyre.M.H., flying Yellow 3 and 4 respectively.	
	8.6.44.	10.40.	BEACH PATROL. Low cover to Neptune. 2 FW 190's were seen North West of Bayuex, otherwise the patrol was uneventful.	
	8.6.44.	14.45.	BEACH PATROL. The Squadron provided low cover to Neptune, and whilst flying in the Caen area saw one FW 190 which dropped its bomb and escaped into cloud before it could be engaged.	
	8.6.44.	19.00.	BEACH PATROL. Whilst providing low cover to Neptune the Squadron encountered 12 + ME 109 Fighter Bombers and 20 + FW 190 Fighter Bombers and engaged same. In the meelee that followed F/O.J.A.Houlton, F/O.A.B.Stead and F/O.F.Transom each destroyed a ME 109, and P/O.H.W.B.Patterson destroyed a FW 190, while S/Ldr J.B.Niven and W/O Esdaile each claimed a FW 190 as damaged, thus making a total of 4 destroyed and 2 damaged for no loss, quite a feather in the cap of the Squadron.	
	9.6.44.	15.40.	BEACH PATROL. The Squadron provided low cover to Neptune East. Quite uneventful.	
	10.6.44.	05.40.	BEACH PATROL. Low cover Neptune East. 2 FW 190's were seen flying low, towards Caen from N2 but they were not engaged.	
	10.6.44.	10.35.	BEACH PATROL. Low Cover Neptune. Uneventful.	

135

135 Airfield

YEAR: 1944 MONTH. DATE.	AIRCRAFT. Type.	No.	PILOT, OR 1ST PILOT.	2ND PILOT, PUPIL, OR PASSENGER.	DUTY (INCLUDING RESULTS AND REMARKS).
—	—	—	—	—	TOTALS BROUGHT FORWARD
JUNE 6	Spitfire IXB	X	Self	—	Beach head patrol - Broken prop solo
6	Spitfire IXB	V	Self	—	Beach head patrol - JU 88's on beaches
6	Spitfire IXB	V	Self	—	Air Test
7	Spitfire IXB	V	Self	—	Beach patrol - chased 190's over fleet
7	Spitfire IXB	V	Self	—	Beach patrol - electrical failure
7	Spitfire IXB	V	Self	—	Beach patrol
8	Spitfire IXB	V	Self	—	Beach patrol
8	Spitfire IXB	V	Self	—	Beach patrol - ME109's & FW.190s on ...
9	Spitfire IXB	V	Self	—	Beach patrol
10	Spitfire IXB	V	Self	—	Beach patrol
10	Spitfire IXB	V	Self	—	Beach patrol
11	Spitfire IXB	V	Self	—	Beach patrol
12	Spitfire IXB	V	Self	—	Beach patrol - ME109 E/B's S of 4Th
13	Spitfire IXB	V	Self	—	Beach patrol - landed in France
13	Spitfire IXB	V	Self	—	Beach patrol - base
15	Spitfire IXB	V	Self	—	Halifaxes & Lancasters on Boulogne
16	Spitfire IXB	V	Self	—	Beach patrol
17	Spitfire IXB	V	Self	—	Beach patrol - burst tyre landed Ft
17	Spitfire IXB	V	Self	—	Ford - base
17	Spitfire IXB	V	Self	—	Beach - patrol
18	Spitfire IXB	V	Self	—	Shipping patrol
19	Spitfire IXB	V	Self	—	Shipping patrol
20	Spitfire IXB	V	Self	—	Beach patrol

GRAND TOTAL [Cols. (1) to (10)].
663 Hrs. **25** Mins.

TOTALS CARRIED FORWARD

SINGLE-ENGINE AIRCRAFT				MULTI-ENGINE AIRCRAFT						PASSEN-GER	INSTR/CLOUD FLYING [Incl. in Cols. (1) to (10)].	
DAY		NIGHT		DAY			NIGHT					
DUAL	PILOT	DUAL	PILOT	DUAL	1ST PILOT	2ND PILOT	DUAL	1ST PILOT	2ND PILOT		DUAL	PILOT
(1)	(2)	(3)	(4)	(5)	(6)	(7)	(8)	(9)	(10)	(11)	(12)	(13)
73.10	538.35	5.45	7.50							20.20	18.30	3.40
	1.40											
卐	1.45	1 Ju 88 destroyed and 1 shared with F/Lt MacDonald, F/O Mayston & F/Sgt Filkins										
	.20											
	1.55											
	.15											
	2.05											
	1.50											
卐	2.05	1 ME 109 des. F/O Transom; P/O Patterson 1 ea. ME 109 destroyed F/O Stead 1 FW 190 des. W/O Esdaile) ea 1 FW 140 S/Ldr Niven) dam}										
	1.45											
	2.10											
	2.00											
	1.55											
卐	1.55	1 ME 109 F/O destroyed. F/Lt Newenham 1 ME 109 P/O destroyed.										
	1.55											
	2.30											
	.20		1.00									
	1.55											
	2.20											
	.20											
	2.10											
	1.50											
	1.50											
	1.25											
73.10	576.40	5.45	7.50							20.20	18.30	3.40
(1)	(2)	(3)	(4)	(5)	(6)	(7)	(8)	(9)	(10)	(11)	(12)	(13)

135 Airfield Selsey

YEAR: 1944	AIRCRAFT.		PILOT, OR 1ST PILOT.	2ND PILOT, PUPIL, OR PASSENGER.	DUTY (INCLUDING RESULTS AND REMARKS).
MONTH	DATE	Type.	No.			
—	—	—	—	—	—	TOTALS BROUGHT FORWARD
June	24	Spitfire IXB	V	Self	—	Beach Patrol
	24	Spitfire IXB	V	Self	—	Beach Patrol
	25	Spitfire IXB	V	Self	—	Halifaxes & Lancasters – No ball Tgt
	27	Spitfire IXB	V	Self	—	Shipping Patrol
	29	Spitfire IXB	V	Self	—	Shipping Patrol
	29	Spitfire IXB	V	Self	—	France to base
	O.R. Hardy OC "B" Flight.	Summary for:- June/44 Unit:- 485 (N.Z.) Sqdn. Aircraft Date:- 30/6/44. Types. Signature:- J.A. Houlton				Spitfire IX B.
July	8	Spitfire IXB	V	Self	—	Air Test
	9	Spitfire IXB	V	Self	—	Halifax Escort
	9	Spitfire IXB	V	Self	—	From Manston.
	12	Spitfire IXB	V	Self	—	Lib Escort
	15	Spitfire IXB	V	Self	—	Lanc Escort - NuCourt
	19	Spitfire IXB	V	Self	—	Lanc Escort
	O.R. Hardy OC "B" Flight	Summary for:- July/44 Unit:- 485 (N.Z.) Sqdn. Aircraft Date:- 31/7/44. Types. Signature:- J.A. Houlton				Spitfire IX B.

GRAND TOTAL [Cols. (1) to (10)]. 652 Hrs. 40 Mins.

TOTALS CARRIED FORWARD

SINGLE-ENGINE AIRCRAFT.		MULTI-ENGINE AIRCRAFT.						PASSEN-GER.	INSTR/CLOUD FLYING [Incl. in Cols. (1) to (10)].	
DAY.		NIGHT.		DAY.			NIGHT.					
DUAL.	PILOT.	DUAL.	PILOT.	DUAL.	1ST PILOT.	2ND PILOT.	DUAL.	1ST PILOT.	2ND PILOT.		DUAL.	PILOT.
(1)	(2)	(3)	(4)	(5)	(6)	(7)	(8)	(9)	(10)	(11)	(12)	(13)
73.10	570.40	5.45	7.50							20.20	18.20	3.40
	2.10											
	2.00											
	1.50											
	1.55											
	2.00											
	.55											
	49.00											
	.50											
	2.10											
	.45											
	1.40											
	2.05											
	1.35											
	9.05											
73.10	595.55	5.45	7.50							20.20	18.20	3.40
(1)	(2)	(3)	(4)	(5)	(6)	(7)	(8)	(9)	(10)	(11)	(12)	(13)

"CO" 485 (NZ) Sqdn

"CO" 485 (NZ) Sqdn

135 WING PERSONAL

COMBAT REPORT No. 16.

- A. June 8th 1944
- B. 485 Squadron
- C. Spitfire IX LF
- D. 19.30 - 20.35.
- E. 20.35
- F. 15 miles W. of Caen
- G. 7000 ft
- H. 6000 ft
- I. Nil
- J. 1 Me 109 destroyed.

F/O. J. HOULTON.

K   I was leading Blue section, patrolling at 5000 ft 15 miles W. of Caen and flying E. E/a were reported by 222 Squadron above the canal S. of Cabourg and I climbed to the S.E. and intercepted 12 + Me 109's flying S below cloud. They were being attacked on the port side by 5 or 6 Spitfires. I singled out the e/a flying on the starboard of the formation, and closing to 300 yards, opened fire from line astern. I saw heavy strikes, pieces flew off and black smoke came from his engine. He porpoised in and out of cloud a few times and as he came out I got in one or two more bursts without effect; on the last occasion, however I followed him up and hit his slip stream in the cloud. I fired again and the black smoke came past me in the cloud. We broke cloud simultaneously and I saw him go down in a shallow dive to crash in a wood. Just before crashing an object came away but no parachute.

     I claim 1 Me 109 destroyed.

....

.... (Intelligence Officer)

135 WING PERSONAL
COMBAT REPORT NO.26.

- A. June 11th 1944.
- B. 485 (New Zealand) Squadron.
- C. Spitfire IX LF
- D. 05.40 - 07.40
- E. 06.40
- F. 2 miles S.W. Aunay - Sur - Odon, Approx. T.8149
- G. Zero ft.
- H. 8000 ft.
- I. Nil
- J. 1 Me 109 Fighter Bomber destroyed.

F/O. J.A. HOULTON.

K.   I was leading Blue Section, flying South about 30 miles S.E. of Omaha Beach at 8000 ft when I saw 2 a/c flying North in line astern on the deck. On diving down upon them, I identified these a/c as Me 109 Fighter-bombers. Closing to 200 yards line astern on the rear e/a, I fired a 3 seconds burst with Cannon and M.G. causing pieces of the a/c to fly off and fire to break out in the engine. E/a then pulled up sharply in flames. At a height of about 600 ft the pilot was thrown clear and his parachute opened. The e/a then crashed and blew up. (Location as above)

The combat was witnessed and the result is confirmed by Blue 3 (P/O. H.W.B. Patterson.) and Blue 4 (F/O. M.C. Mayston.)

I claim this Me 109 Fighter Bomber as destroyed.

..... J A Houlton ..... F/O.

..... G. C. Murray ..... F/O. (Intelligence Officer)

135 WING PERSONAL

COMBAT REPORT.   No. 28.

A. June 29th 1944.
B. 485 (New Zealand) Squadron.
C. Spitfire IX LF
D. 07.35 - 11.30 (after landing France)
E. 0.8.30 approx.
F. 15 miles S. Caen.
G. 10,000 ft.
H. 9,000 ft.
I. Nil.
J. 1 Me 109 Damaged.

K.   F/O. J.A. HOULTON.

I was leading Blue section flying North, 15 miles S. of Caen at 9,000 ft when 12 Me 109's passed over me at 10,000 ft flying South. I broke in behind these e/a which pulled up into cloud except one straggler which took violent evasive action. Firing several short bursts at 300 - 200 yards from varying angles astern, at this E/A I observed strikes on starboard wing root and fuselage before e/a entered cloud.

I claim this Me 109 as damaged.

.... F/O.

.... F/O. Intelligence
                                    Officer.

OPERATIONS RECORD BOOK

DETAIL OF WORK CARRIED OUT

By No. 349 (Belgian) Squadron.

For the Month of February, 1945.

SECRET

APPENDIX

R.A.F. Form 541.

Page No. 2

Date	Aircraft Type & Number	Crew	Duty	Time Up	Time Down	Details of Sortie or Flight	References
9.2.45. (contd.)	Spitfire IX LF. ML 407	F/L A.CLAESEN.	Recce'	11.40	11.45		
	MK 717	F/S BRANDERS L.					
	NH 551	F/L G.SEYDEL.		12.55	13.40		
	MK 804	F/O P.ERKES.					
	ML 407	F/L A.CLAESEN.		12.20	13.35		
	MK 717	F/S BRANDERS L.					
	NH 323	F/O J.CROJET.		14.55	15.55		
	NH 538	F/S BRANDERS H.			16.00		
	ML 407	F/L A.CLAESEN.		16.05	17.15		
	MK 717	F/S BRANDERS L.					
	NH 487	F/L MYCROFT.		17.15	18.10		
	MK 804	F/O A.VANDERHEYDEN.					
10.2.45.	ML 365	W/O A.UYDENS.	Recce'	14.35	16.45	DD.639. Armed recce ZWOLLE-AMERSFOORT-ELBRICH-ENSCHEDE. 1 hutted camp straffed, 1 MET damaged.	
	NH 311	F/S SHERDON D.			16.25		
	ML 717	F/L MYCROFT M.		14.30			
	MK 804	F/O A.VANDERHEYDEN.					
	ML 407	F/L A.CLAESEN.		15.05	16.40		
	MK 799	F/S BRANDERS L.			16.30		
	NH 323	F/O J.CROJET.		15.15	16.25		
	NH 425	F/S LACOSTE J.			16.35		
11.2.45.	NH 487	F/L J.WOOD.	Recce'	08.15	09.00	DD.667. Armed recce' ROTTERDAM-AMERSFOORT-ARNHEM areas, 1 loco destroyed at D.8898.	
	NH 323	F/O J.CROJET.		08.05			
	NH 551	F/L G.SEYDEL.		08.10	09.05		
	ML 407	F/O S.TUCK.					
	NH 311	F/S SHERDON D.		08.20	09.00		
	NH 425	F/S LEROY N.					
	MK 804	F/L M.MYCROFT.		08.35	09.15		
	MK 717	F/S BRANDERS L.					
	NH 487	F/L J.WOOD.	Weather recce'	11.10	12.00	Weather recce'. Battle areas, uneventful.	
	NH 311	F/S SHERDON D.					
13.2.45	NH 487	F/L J.WOOD.	Recce'.	08.55	10.10	D.697. Armed recce' area V. Road straffing. 2 MET destroyed and 3 damaged, 3 H.D.V. damaged, 4 locos damaged.	
	NH 311	F/S LACOSTE J.			10.20		
	ML 365	F/C A.UYDENS.		09.20	10.20		
	NH 425	W/S BRANDERS H.			10.15		
	MK 804	F/C P.ERKES.		09.05	10.30		
	ML 407	F/S BRANDERS L.			09.50		
	MK 717	F/L M.MYCROFT.		09.30	10.25		
	MK 799	F/C A.VANDERHEYDEN.			10.15		
	NH 487	F/S SHERDON D.		11.05	12.00	D.697. ditto. 4 MET destroyed and 5 damaged, 1 H.D.T. destroyed and 6 damaged.	
	NH 425	F/S BRANDERS H.					
	NH 323	F/O J.CROJET.		11.50	12.40		
	NH 311	F/S LACOSTE J.					
	MK 804	F/O P.ERKES.			12.45		
	ML 407	F/S VAN HAMME A.			13.00		
	NH 551	F/L M.MYCROFT.		12.05	13.35		
	MK 799	F/O A.VANDERHEYDEN.					

AIRCRAFT (HEAVIER-THAN-AIR).

1. Nationality and Registration Marks EIRE. No. 162.

2. Classification of Aircraft : Category .... Sub-division

3. Owner :— REPUBLIC OF EIRE AIR CORPS.
   Name ~~Vickers Armstrongs Ltd~~
   Address BALDONNEL.
   ~~Nationality~~ EIRE.
   ~~Authority~~ ~~21/9/10601~~

4. Constructor VICKERS - ARMSTRONGS LIMITED,
   SUPERMARINE WORKS, SOUTHAMPTON.

5. Type of Aircraft SPITFIRE 'F' MARK 9.   6. Constructor's No. ~~ML-407~~ CBAF 2111.

7. Maximum total weight authorised

8. Weight—empty

9. Maximum commercial load authorised when fuel and oil tanks are full

10. Engine(s) Type MERLIN MARK 66   Series No.(s) ~~194013~~ ~~A4888UU~~ 186327/A A83001

11. Airscrew(s) Type R.12/4F5/4 Serial No. VA.8351 ~~H5605~~   Pitch 22° 20' Diameter 10' 9"
    Maker's name ROTOL LIMITED. ~~Hoover Ltd~~

12. Type of wireless apparatus TRANSMITTER RECEIVER STR 9×2.

(From Ministry of Civil Aviation Airframe Log Book for ML 407. Courtesy of Irish Air Corps.)

YEAR 1951 MONTH / DATE	AIRCRAFT Type	No.	PILOT, OR 1ST PILOT	2ND PILOT, PUPIL OR PASSENGER	DUTY (INCLUDING RESULTS AND REMARKS)
—	—	—	—	—	TOTALS BROUGHT FORWARD
July 29	Anson	141	Lt Coughlin	Self	Baldonnel to Eastleigh
" 30	Spitfire	162	Self	—	Eastleigh to Speke
" 30	"	162	Self	—	Speke to Baldonnel
Aug 8	"	158	Self	—	G. F. P. & Aerobatics
" 13	"	159	Self	—	" " "
" 9	Magister	128	Self	Pte Bayle	To Gormanston
" 9	"	128	"	"	To Baldonnel via Dundalk

FLYING TIME : MONTH ENDING 25.8.51
PILOT 4 H 15 M   2nd PILOT — H — M
DUAL — H — M   PASSENGER 2 H 20 M
TOTAL TIME IN AIR : 6 H 35 M
CHECKED [signature] Capt.
CERTIFIED
O.C. AIR CORPS

| Sept 21 | Magister | 136 | Self | — | Baldonnel to Gormanston |
| " 21 | Seafire | 157 | Self | — | Oblique Photography |

FLYING TIME : MONTH ENDING 29.9.51
PILOT 1 H 30 M   2nd PILOT — H — M
DUAL — H — M   PASSENGER — H — M
TOTAL TIME IN AIR : 1 H 30 M
CHECKED [signature] Capt.
CERTIFIED
O.C. AIR CORPS

GRAND TOTAL [Cols. (1) to (10)]
945 Hrs. 50 Mins.

TOTALS CARRIED FORWARD

Date		Aircraft	Reg	Pilot	Details		
	31	C182	GATCX	Self	PARA DROPPING		
APRIL	16	SPITFIRE MKIXT	GLFIX	Self	TEST FLIGHT (INITIAL FLIGHT)		
	20	SPITFIRE MKIXT	GLFIX	Self	— —		
	23	SPIT.F.IX MKIXT	GLFIX	Self	ST MERRYN PLYMOUTH BOURNEMOUTH	MIDDLE WALLOP	
	24	SPITFIRE MKIXT	GLFIX	Self	COMPASS SWING MIDI. WALLOP + TEST.		
	25	ML407	GLFIX	Self	M/WALLOP BOURNEMOUTH ST MERRYN		
MAY	1st	ML407	GLFIX	Self	ST MERRYN LOCAL TEST		
	3	ML407	GLFIX	Self	ST MERRYN - ST JUST ST MERRYN.		
	28"	ML407	GLFIX	Self	ST MERRYN BOURNEMOUTH GOODWOOD		
	29	ML407	GLFIX	Self	GOODWOOD ST MERRYN		
JUNE	1	DH104	GBLB2	Self	ST MERRYN ST JUST ST MERRYN.		
	8	ML407	GLFIX	Self	LOCAL		
	9	ML407	GLFIX	Self	ST MERRYN GOODWOOD ST MERRYN		
	10	BH104	GBLB2	Self	ST MERRYN ST JUST		
	12	STAMPE	GAXNW	Self	NEWBURY ST MERRYN		
	14	ML407	GLFIX	Self	LOCAL TEST.		

Date	Aircraft	Reg	Pilot		Route		Start	End
15.7.90	Stampe	GAXNW	Self	P1	Whitewaltham	Local	11.15	11.3
15.7.90	Stampe	GAXNW	Self	P1	Whitewaltham	Local	15.10	15.1
15.7.90	Stampe	GAXNW	Self	P1	Whitewaltham	Local	16.00	16.15
15.7.90	Stampe	GAXNW	Self	P1	Whitewaltham	Goodwood	17.30	17.5
17.7.90	Spitfire	GLFIX	Self	P1	Whitewaltham	Local	11.55	12.05
17.7.90	Spitfire	GLFIX	Self	P1	Whitewaltham	Local	12.10	12.2
17.7.90	Spitfire	GLFIX	Self	P1	Whitewaltham	Local	13.00	13.3
21.7.90	Stampe	GAXNW	Self	P1	Goodwood	Local	17.05	17.2
21.7.90	Stampe	GAXNW	Self	P1	Goodwood	Local	17.40	18.0
29.7.90	Spitfire	GLFIX	Self	P1	Goodwood	Local	16.10	16.30

			1.05								
			.20								
			.25								
Radio			1.10								
			1.20								
			1.15								
			1.10								
			2.35								
			2.30								
			.50								
										2.20	
			1.15								
			3.20								
										1.05	
			2.10								
			1.30								

.20									Local
.35									Local
.15									Local + formation
.25									X Country
.10									Circuits PK
.10									Circuits PK
.35*									*Formation-solo!!!
.15									Local Olivia
.25									Local Richard
.20									Local Xwind PK

Appendix 2: Operational Flights of ML 407
(According to Squadron Operations Record Books)

485 (NZ) Squadron – 135 Wing   Squadron ID code "OU-V"

A.L.G. Selsey		Up-Down	Duty	
01.05.44	F/O J.A. Houlton	1805-1855	Ramrod (escort)	-
07.05.44	F/Lt K.J. Macdonald	1110-1255	"	-
07.05.44	F/Sgt R.M. Clarke	1850-2030	"	-
08.05.44	F/Lt K.J. Macdonald	0910-1100	"	-
09.05.44	F/O J.A. Houlton	0955-1100	"	-
09.05.44	F/Lt K.J. Macdonald	1830-1940	"	-
10.05.44	F/O J.A. Houlton	1515-1700	"	-
15.05.44	"	0810-1035	"	-
20.05.44	"	1000-1120	Ramrod (bombing)	-
20.05.44	"	1555-1720	"	Ski site
21.05.44	F/Lt K.C. Lee	1040-1215	Ramrod	MET attacked
22.05.44	F/O J.A. Houlton	1855-2035	Ranger	"
24.05.44	F/Sgt R.M. Clarke	1100-1220	Ramrod (bombing)	Ski site
30.05.44	F/O J.A. Houlton	1025-1140	"	"
06.06.44	"	1850-1955	Beach Patrol	D-Day (Neptune)
07.06.44	"	1035-1050	"	(Neptune)
07.06.44	"	1900-2105	"	"
08.06.44	W/Cdr P.J. Simpson	0540-0550	"	"
08.06.44	F/O J.A. Houlton	1040-1230	"	"
08.06.44	"	1900-2105	"	Me 109 destroyed
09.06.44	"	1540-1725	"	(Neptune)
10.06.44	"	1035-1245	"	"
10.06.44	"	1445-1645	"	"
11.06.44	F/Lt K.C. Lee	0540-0735	"	"
11.06.44	F/O J.A. Houlton	1040-1245	"	"
12.06.44	"	0540-0735	"	Me 109 destroyed
12.06.44	F/Lt K.C. Lee	1900-2100	"	(Neptune)
13.06.44	F/O J.A. Houlton	0625-0820	"	Down B.3 (St Croix-sur-Mer)
13.06.44	"	1040-1220	"	Back to Selsey
14.06.44	F/Lt K.C. Lee	2130-2340	"	(Neptune)
15.06.44	F/Lt W.A. Newenham	1305-1345	"	"
15.06.44	F/O J.A. Houlton	2210-2330	Ramrod (escort)	-
17.06.44	"	0740-0950	Beach Patrol	-
17.06.44	"	1505-1715	"	-
19.06.44	"	0805-0955	Shipping Patrol	-
19.06.44	F/Lt K.C. Lee	1715-1840	"	-
19.06.44	W/O D.F. Clarke	2055-2220	Bombing	Noball target
20.06.44	F/O J.A. Houlton	1430-1555	Escort	-
20.06.44	P/O H.W.B. Patterson	1959-2210	Beach Patrol	-
22.06.44	F/Lt K.C. Lee	0820-1020	"	-
22.06.44	F/Lt K.J. Macdonald	1520-1725	"	-
23.06.44	"	0820-1030	"	-
24.06.44	F/Lt K.C. Lee	0920-1125	"	-
24.06.44	F/O J.A. Houlton	1420-1630	"	-

Date	Pilot	Time	Duty	Notes
24.06.44	"	2020-2220	Beach Patrol	-
25.06.44	"	0815-1005	Escort	-
27.06.44	"	1725-1940	Beach Patrol	-
29.06.44	"	0730-0930	"	Me 109 damaged
29.06.44	F/Lt K.J. Macdonald	1330-1525	"	-
29.06.44	F/Lt K.C. Lee	1925-2125	"	Landed B.2 (Bazenville)
30.06.44	"	0525-0635	"	-
30.06.44	"	0840-1010	"	Back to base

A.L.G. Coolham

Date	Pilot	Up-Down	Duty	
01.07.44	W/O D.F. Clarke	1630-1830	Ramrod (escort)	-
03.07.44	F/O T.S.F. Kearins	2025-2240	"	-

A.L.G. Funtington

Date	Pilot	Up-Down	Duty	
04.07.44	F/Lt K.J. Macdonald	1325-1435	"	-
06.07.44	"	1205-1425	"	-
06.07.44	"	2015-2140	"	-
09.07.44	F/O J.A. Houlton	1220-1430	"	-
12.07.44	"	0715-0855	"	-
12.07.44	F/Lt K.C. Lee	1910-2135	"	-
15.07.44	F/O J.A. Houlton	1535-1740	"	-
16.07.44	W/O A.J. Downer	1900-2100	"	-
18.07.44	F/O T.S.F. Kearins	0520-0715	"	-
19.07.44	F/O J.A. Houlton	1525-1700	"	-
20.07.44	P/O H.W.B. Patterson	2010-2200	"	-
22.07.44	"	1655-1750	"	-
24.07.44	F/O T.S.F. Kearins	1050-1105	"	-
25.07.44	W/O A.J. Downer	0830-1000	"	-
25.07.44	"	1900-2105	"	-
27.07.44	F/Sgt R.M. Clarke	1915-2040	"	-
28.07.44	W/O A.J. Downer	1700-1850	"	-
28.07.44	"	2040-2150	"	-
30.07.44	W/O A.J. Downer	0720-0845	"	-
30.07.44	F/Lt K.J. Macdonald	1415-1605	"	-
31.07.44	W/O D.F. Clarke	1915-2145	"	Landed B.12 (Ellon)

B.12 Ellon

Date	Pilot	Up-Down	Duty	
01.08.44	F/O F. Transom	1955-2140	Ramrod (target cover)	-
02.08.44	F/Lt L.M. Ralph	1625-1825	Ramrod (escort)	-
03.08.44	S/Ldr J.B. Niven	1920-2100	Ramrod (target cover)	-
04.08.44	W/O A.J. Downer	1220-1425	Ramrod (close escort)	-

A.L.G. Selsey

Date	Pilot	Up-Down	Duty	
10.08.44	F/O J.A. Houlton	1100-1115	Ramrod (escort)	-
11.08.44	F/O R.H. de Tourret	1545-1755	Ramrod (target cover)	-
12.08.44	F/O J.A. Houlton	1240-1250	Ramrod (top cover)	-
13.08.44	F/O T.S.F. Kearins	0910-1120	Ramrod (patrol)	-
14.08.44	F/O J.A. Houlton	0930-1130	Ramrod (close escort)	-
14.08.44	F/O A.B. Stead	1830-2010	Ramrod (escort)	-

Bradwell Bay

Date	Pilot	Up-Down	Duty	
15.08.44	F/O A.B. Stead	1105-1325	Ramrod (escort)	-

15.08.44	W/O D.F. Clarke	1750-1910	Ramrod (target cover)	-
16.08.44	"	0725-0840	"	-

R.A.F. Tangmere — Up-Down — Duty

19.08.44	F/O R.H. de Tourret	1150-1250	Armed Recce	-
20.08.44	F/O F. Transom	1125-1225	"	-
23.08.44	F/O T.S.F. Kearins	1930-2025	Rodeo (sweep)	-
24.08.44	"	0640-0830	Sweep	-
25.08.44	D.F. Clarke	1930-2130	Ramrod (escort cover)	-
26.08.44	F/O J.A. Houlton	0925-1135	Ramrod (close escort)	-
26.08.44	F/O F. Transom	1810-2025	Ramrod (area escort)	-

Bradwell Bay — Up-Down — Duty

27.08.44	F/O J.A. Houlton	1250-1540	Ramrod (escort)	-

B.17 Carpiquet — Up-Down — Duty

31.08.44	F/O J.A. Houlton	2000-2220	Armed Recce	-
01.09.44	F/O L.S.M. White	1520-1705	Recce	-

B.35 Godelemesnil (Eu) — Up-Down — Duty

11.09.44	P/O H.W.B. Patterson	1255-1435	Fighter Recce	-
15.09.44	F/O A.B. Stead	1340-1425	Dive Bombing	-
16.09.44	F/Lt O.L. Hardy	0915-0955	"	-
17.09.44	W/O A.J. Downer	1520-1555	"	-
17.09.44	F/O A.B. Stead	1815-1915	"	-
20.09.44	W/O A.J. Downer	1100-1140	"	-

B.53 Merville — Up-Down — Duty

23.09.44	F/O A.B. Stead	1620-1750	Dive Bombing	-
26.09.44	F/Lt W.A. Newenham	1530-1625	"	-
27.09.44	F/O A.B. Stead	1025-1055	"	-
28.09.44	"	0925-1100	"	-
28.09.44	"	1610-1705	"	-
02.10.44	"	1025-1200	Armed Recce	-
02.10.44	F/O M.C. Mayston	1645-1800	Dive Bombing	-
12.10.44	F/O A. Roberts	1025-1145	"	-
17.10.44	F/O A.B. Stead	0845-0955	"	-
17.10.44	F/Sgt P.T. Humphrey	1215-1330	"	-
17.10.44	F/O A.B. Stead	1440-1515	"	-
18.10.44	F/Lt J.N. King	1130-1250	"	-
19.10.44	F/O M.C. Mayston	1045-1210	"	-
21.10.44	W/O E.G. Atkins	1415-1540	"	-
29.10.44	F/O A.B. Stead	1530-1625	"	-

B.65 Maldegem — Up-Down — Duty

01.11.44	F/O A.B. Stead	1030-1150	Shipping Cover	-
01.11.44	F/Lt J.N. King	1430-1600	"	-
02.11.44	F/O A.B. Stead	1245-1345	Dive Bombing	-
04.11.44	"	1435-1530	"	-
30.11.44	"	1020-1215	Armed Recce	MET attacked
30.11.44	F/O M.C. Mayston	1605-1645	Nickelling	Leaflet raid

Date	Pilot	Up-Down	Duty	
03.12.44	F/O A.B. Stead	0955-1120	Dive Bombing	-
04.12.44	F/O M.C. Mayston	1915-2015	"	-
04.12.44	W/O Downer	1400-1455	"	-
06.12.44	F/O M.C. Mayston	1230-1410	Fighter Cover	-
08.12.44	F/O A.B. Stead	0910-1035	Dive Bombing	-
10.12.44	"	1315-1445	"	-
11.12.44	F/Lt O.L. Hardy	0915-0945	Escort	-
11.12.44	F/O A.B. Stead	1430-1535	"	-
15.12.44	F/O A. Roberts	1115-1350	"	-
23.12.44	W/O A.J. Downer	1145-1350	Fighter Patrol	-
23.12.44	"	1455-1655	"	-
24.12.44	W/O W.A. Hoskins	1210-1300	Sweep	3 jet a/c seen
25.12.44	W/O A.J. Downer	0935-1130	"	Me 262 seen
26.12.44	"	1440-1555	Target Cover	2 Me 262s engaged by Squadron
28.12.44	P/O R.M. Clarke	1420-1525	Fighter Sweep	-
29.12.44	"	1215-1410	"	Me 262 seen
29.12.44	"	1505-1615	Area Cover	-
31.12.44	P/O R.M. Clarke	1115-1305	Area Cover	-

In February Squadron withdrawn to Predannack to covert to Tempests.

341 (FF) Squadron – 145 Wing   Squadron ID code "NL-D"

B.70 Deurne/Antwerp

Date	Pilot	Up-Down	Duty	
29.12.44	Sgt C. Alépée	1340-1505	Fighter Support	-
31.12.44	Sgt J. Dabos	0840-1025	"	-
01.01.45	"	1010-1200	Scramble	Response to Bodenplatte
01.01.45	"	1430-1545	Fighter Support	-

05.01.45 Squadron released from ops.

308 (Polish) Squadron – 131 Wing   Squadron ID code "ZF-R"

B.50 Grimbergen

Date	Pilot	Up-Down	Duty
22.01.45	F/O W. Stanski	0840-1005	Weather Recce
24.01.45	W/O J. Sawoszczyk	1330-1450	Dive Bombing

Squadron continued on ops.

349 (Belgian) Squadron – 135 Wing   Squadron ID code "GE-P"

B.77 Gilze Rijen

Date	Pilot	Up-Down	Duty	
08.02.45	F/Lt A. Claesen	1400-1550	Recce	MET Destroyed
08.02.45	F/Sgt D. Smerdon	1410-1600	"	- *
09.02.45	F/Lt G. Seydel	0755-0945	"	-
09.02.45	F/Lt A. Claesen	1140-1145	"	-
09.02.45	"	1220-1355	"	-
09.02.45	"	1605-1715	"	-
10.02.45	"	1505-1640	"	-
11.02.45	F/O S. Tuck	0810-0905	"	-

13.02.45	F/Sgt L. Branders	0905-0950	Recce		-
13.02.45	F/Sgt A. Hamme	1150-1300	"		-

Squadron withdrawn to Predannack to convert to Tempests.

345 (FF) Squadron – 145 Wing   Squadron ID code "2Y-A"

B.85 Schijndel   *Up-Down*   *Duty*

28.02.45	Lt Seguy	1015-1110	red	(patrol and interdiction)
01.03.45	Comdt Guizard	0705-0815	"	-
02.03.45	"	1020-1125	blue	-
05.03.45	"	0825-0915	red	-
09.03.45	"	0950-1040	"	-
13.03.45	"	1120-1300	"	-
13.03.45	Capt Guérin	1640-1730	blue	-
15.03.45				to B.84 Rips
17.03.45				to Fairwood Common
03.04.45				to B.85 Schijndel

B.85 Schijndel   *Up-Down*   *Duty*

04.04.45	Comdt Guizard	0655-0815	red	(armed recces and escorts)
07.04.45	,,	0710-0840	yellow	-
08.04.45	Lt de Bouillane	1545-1755	"	-
08.04.45	Lt Harmel	1900-2100	orange	-
12.04.45	Lt Gelly	0925-1120	red	-
12.04.45	Comdt Guizard	1505-1645	white	-
13.04.45	Lt Le Boëtté	1455-1555	red	-

April 1945 re-equipped with Spitfire LF XVI, continued on ops.

322 (Norge) Squadron — 132 Wing Squadron ID code "AH-B"

B.85 Schijndel   *Up-Down*   *Duty*

16.04.45	Sgt R. Anonsen	1500-1615	Armed Recce	-

B.106 Twenthe   *Up-Down*   *Duty*

19.04.45	Sgt E. Stigset	1000-1130	Patrol	-
19.04.45	Lt J. Rosland	1240-1410	"	-
19.04.45	Sgt R. Anonsen	1515-1700	"	-
21.04.45	Sgt E. Stigset	1830-1945	Armed Recce	-

22.04.45 Squadron withdrawn from ops to Scotland, en route for home — Norway.

485 (NZ) Squadron — 132 Wing   Squadron ID code "OU-B"

22.04.45 acquired from 332 Squadron, no recorded ops.

Significant quotes for ML 407 from 485 Squadron Operations Record Book

21.05.44 up 10.40 down 12.15

Flight Lieutenant Lee (Blue 1) and Flying Officer Stead (Blue 2) attacked a tracked Vehicle which is confirmed destroyed.

22.05.44 up 18.55 down 20.35

Four members of the Squadron took part in a Ranger to the Eindhoven area. Two heavy tanks believed to have been Mk V or, VI stationary at D5935 were attacked, damaged and left in smoke. At D5044 a Troop bus was attacked and the roof blown off. A party of Troops on cycles were also shot up. . .

08.06.44 Beach Patrol up 19.00 down 21.05

Whilst providing low cover to Neptune the Squadron encountered 12+ Me 109 Fighter Bombers and engaged same. In the melée that followed F/O J.A. Houlton, F/O A.B. Stead and P/O Transom each destroyed a Me 109, and P/O H.W.B Patterson destroyed a Fw 190, while S/Ldr J.B. Niven and W/O H.M. Esdaile each claimed a Fw 190 as damaged, thus making a total of 4 destroyed and 2 damaged for no loss, quite a feather in the cap of the Squadron.

12.06.44 Beach Patrol up 05.40 down 07.35

Whilst patrolling at approximately T.85 2 Me 109's were seen flying North at zero feet. These two enemy destroyed by F/O J.A. Houlton and F/Lt. W.A. Newenham flying Blue 1 and 2 respectively.

13.06.44 Beach Patrol up 06.25 down 08.20

The Squadron took off to provide low cover to Neptune, and at the conclusion of their mission landed in France at R & R Strip B.3., from which they took off to perform their next duty.

29.06.44 Beach Patrol up 07.30 down 09.30

Low cover was provided by the Squadron in the Assault area. 4 Fw 190's were met N.E. of Caen at 10,000 feet apparently on patrol and were engaged without result. 12 Me 109's were met 10 miles S.E. Caen flying South on patrol at 10,000 feet. One enemy aircraft was damaged by F/O Houlton. MET approximately 10 miles S.E Caen attacked, strikes were observed and a vehicle was ditched. Afterwards the Squadron was unsuccessfully bounced by 2 Me 109's. Three aircraft landed in France and then returned to base.

30.11.44 Armed Recce up 10.20 down 12.15

Three aircraft participated in an Armed Recce, and attacked MET claiming 4 Flamers, 2 Smokers and 5 damaged. Quite a good show.

Appendix 3: Movement Record 1944-1994

Type of Aircraft: Supermarine Type 361 Spitfire LF IXc (with "e" wing armament)
Contractor: Vickers-Armstrongs, Castle Bromwich
Contract Number: B 981687/39
Engine: Rolls-Royce Merlin 66
Construction number: CBAF 2111 (firewall no. CBAF 8463)
RAF serial number: ML 407

23.04.44	taken on charge 33 MU (Maintenance Unit), Lyneham
29.04.44	delivered by ATA to 485 (New Zealand) Sqd, 135 Airfield Selsey
30.04.44	taken on charge 485 (New Zealand) Sqd, 135 Airfield Selsey as "OU-V"
01.05.44	first operational sortie with 485 (New Zealand) Sqd
06.06.45	new propeller fitted
30.06.44	to ALG Coolham
04.07.44	to ALG Funtington
07.08.44	to ALG Selsey
19.08.44	to RAF Station Tangmere
31.08.44	to B.17 Caen/Carpiquet (France)
07.09.44	to B.35 Eu (France)
12.09.44	to B.53 Merville (France)
12.10.44	Category AC Flying Battle damage
19.10.44	Re-categorised A
02.11.44	to B.65 Maldegem (Belgium)
08.11.44	to Fairwood Common (APC)
25.11.44	to B.65 Maldegem (Belgium)
30.11.44	to 420 RSU (Repair & Salvage Unit), B.60 Grimbergen (Belgium)
11.12.44	to 485 (New Zealand) Sqd, B.65 Maldegem
28.12.44	to 145 (Free French) Wing, B.70 Antwerp/Deurne (Belgium)
29.12.44	first operational sortie with 341 (Free French) Sqd as "NL-D"
04.01.45	transferred from 341 (Free French) Sqd
04.01.45	transferred to 131 (Polish) Wing, B.61 St Denijs Westrem/Gent (Belgium)
11.01.45	taken on charge 308 (Polish) Sqd as "ZF-R"
14.01.45	to B.60, Grimbergen
22.01.45	first operational sortie with 308 (Polish) Sqd
08.02.45	transferred to 135 Wing, B.77 Gilze-Rijen (Neth.), taken on charge 349 (Belge) Sqd as "GE-P"
08.02.45	first operational sortie with 349 (Belge) Sqd
19.02.45	probably left in charge of 485 (New Zealand) Sqd, B.77 Gilze-Rijen
22.02.45	transferred from 485 (New Zealand) Sqd to 145 (Free French) Wing
28.02.45	first operational sortie with 345 (Free French) Sqd, B.85 Schijndel, as "2Y-A"
16.03.45	to Fairwood Common (APC)
22.03.45	taken on charge 345 (Free French) Sqd
02.04.45	to B.85 Schijndel
16.04.45	first operational sortie with 332 (Norge) Sqd, B.85 Schijndel, 132 (Norge) Wing as "AH-B"
19.04.45	taken on charge 332 (Norge) Sqd
20.04.45	to Twenthe (Netherlands)
22.04.45	acquired by 485 (NZ) Sqdn, B.106 Twenthe as "OU-B"
26.04.45	485 (NZ) Sqd to 151 RU (Repair Unit), B.55 Wevelgem (Belgium). 204 hours 45 minutes on 174 operations flown. Merlin 66 194013/A.488844 probably fitted at 400-hour check
26.08.45	test-flown after overhaul at 151 RU
22.09.45	airframe total time 319 hours 50 minutes

27.09.45	taken on charge 29 MU High Ercall (storage depot)
00.03.46	registered in Home Census
29.12.49	registered in Home Census
19.07.50	sold to Vickers Armstrongs as non-effective aircraft
00.10.50	received at Vickers-Armstrongs, Eastleigh, for conversion to (two-seat) Fighter Trainer
18.07.51	Merlin 66, 186327/A.483001 test-run (probably replacing Merlin 66, 194013/A.488844) new propeller fitted
24.07.51	first test-flight with number G.15-175, at Eastleigh, after conversion
30.07.51	acceptance-flight, sale and ferry-flight to Irish Air Corps with serial number "162"
25.08.51	taken on charge by "B" Flight Schools (Baldonnel)
01.03.57	400-hour check, engine 308113 fitted
26.04.57	transferred to "A" Flight No. 1 Fighter Sqd (Gormanston)
28.07.58	to Flight Schools
28.02.59	to No. 1 Fighter Sqd
31.03.59	to Flight Schools
08.07.60	last flight with IAC, relegated to instructional airframe at Baldonnel, total time 1082 hours 25 minutes
04.03.68	sold by IAC to Mr N.A.W. Samuelson, Samuelson Films, stored Cricklewood
00.04.70	sold to Sir William Roberts, Shoreham
23.04.70	spares moved from Cricklewood to Shoreham, airframe to Flimwell
19.03.71	airframe to Shoreham
05.10.71	moved back to Flimwell
02.03.72	moved to Strathallan Aircraft collection, Auchterarder
09.08.79	sold to Nick Grace on behalf of Island Trading Ltd
29.10.79	moved to St Merryn for restoration to airworthiness
01.02.80	registered with Civil Aviation Authority (to Island Trading Ltd) as "G-LFIX"
16.04.85	first flight after restoration at St Merryn (with Rolls-Royce Merlin 25, 150571 and new propeller)
04.09.85	St Merryn to Middle Wallop
16.01.86	Middle Wallop to Southampton (Eastleigh)
05.03.86	wheels-up landing, Eastleigh
25.03.86	damage repaired and ready for flight, Eastleigh
25.07.86	Southampton to Goodwood
23.09.90	Goodwood to Duxford
06.03.92	Merlin 25, 439755 fitted 364 hours 55 minutes since rebuild

NB: Where dates do not agree with the 41 Group (RAF) Movement Card they are drawn from Operations Record Books or pilot's Log Books.

Appendix 4: List of Sources

Books

"Aircraft of the Fighting Powers Vol. 6", Owen Thetford — Argus 1979
"An Illustrated History of the New Zealand Spitfire Squadron", Kevin W. Wells — Hutchinson (NZ) 1984
"The Battle of the Airfields", N. L. R. Franks — William Kimber 1982
"British Aviation Colours", John Tanner — Arms & Armour 1976
"The British Fighter Since 1912", Peter Lewis — Putnam 1979
"Combat Aircraft of the World", John W. R. Taylor — Ebury Press & Michael Joseph 1969
"Dutch Spitfires, a Technical Study", Harry van der Meer & Theo Melchers — Repro Holland bv 1988
"Fighter", Len Deighton — Jonathan Cape 1977
"Fighter Squadrons of the RAF", John D. R. Rawlins — Macdonald & Jane's 1969
"Green Kiwi versus German Eagle", J. Norby King — Author Published (NZ) 1991
"The Forgotten Pilots", Lettice Curtis — Curtis 1971
"The Lore of Flight", John Taylor (Ed.) — Thomas Nelson 1973
"Ominous Skies", Harald Penrose — HMSO 1980
"The Peenemünde Raid", Martin Middlebrook — Allen Lane 1982
"Pilots Notes for the Spitfire IX, XI & XVI" — Air Data
"The Right of the Line", John Terraine — Hodder & Stoughton 1985
"Sigh for a Merlin", Alex Henshaw — John Murray 1979
"Spitfire", Roy Cross & Gerald Scarborough — Patrick Stephens 1971
"Spitfire a Documentary History", Alfred Price — Jane's
"Spitfire a Test Pilot's Story", Jeffrey Quill — John Murray 1983
"Spitfire at War", Alfred Price — Ian Allen 1978
"The Spitfire Story", Alfred Price — Jane's 1982
"Spitfire Survivors", Gordon Riley & Graham Trant — Aston Publications 1986
"Spitfire. The History", Eric B. Morgan & Edward Shacklady — Key Publishing 1987
"Spitfire the Story of a Famous Fighter", Bruce Robertson — Harleyford 1960
"Spitfire Strikes", Johnnie Houlton — John Murray 1985
"Strategy for Defeat – the Luftwaffe 1933-1945", Williamson Murray — Airpower Research Institute 1983
"Supermarine Aircraft Since 1914", C. F. Andrews & E. B. Morgan — Putnam 1981
"Supermarine Spitfire", Chaz Bowyer — Bison 1981
"2194 Days of War", Salmaggi & Pallavisini — W. H. Smith & Son 1979
"Victory in the West", L. F. Ellis — HMSO 1968

Periodicals

"Air International" March 1985 "Spitfire: Simply Superb"
"Aeroplane Monthly" January-April 1979 "Anything to Anywhere", Lettice Curtis
"FlyPast" No. 102, January 1990 "A Promise is a Promise", Hugh Smallwood
"FlyPast" No. 150, January 1994 "Going Solo", Ken Ellis
"Profile" Number 221 "Supermarine Seafires (Merlins)", Len Batchelor
"Scale Aircraft Modelling" Vol. 3 No. 10 1981 "The Irish Air Corps", Anthony P Kearns

Video-tapes

"Perfect Lady", Graham Hurley (Solo Enterprises)
"Going Solo", Graham Hurley (Solo Enterprises)

Archive and unpublished

Bradley, Peter "Memoirs of the War" (Ms, 1944)
Collett, M. A. "The Personal War Diary of NZ 422260 Flying Officer M.A. Collett" (Ms)

Imperial War Museum, Lambeth (Printed Books, Documents, Photographic and Film Libraries)
Public Records Office, Kew (AIR 26: Wing Operations Record Books, AIR 27: Squadron Operations Record Books, AIR 29: Maintenance Units Operations Record Books, AIR 50: Individual Combat Reports, AVIA 18: A & AEE Reports)
RAF Air Historical Branch, Kingsway, London (Movement Cards and Accident Records)
Roddis, Joe *"My Memories of my Time with 485 (NZ) Spitfire Squadron"* (Ms, 1994)
Rolls-Royce Ltd, Derby, (Library Archive)
RAF Museum, Hendon (Department of Research & Information Services)
Vickers Ltd, London (Company papers)
Polish Institute and Sikorski Museum, London

Aircrew records

Armée de l'Air, BCIAAA, Chartres, France
Association Nationale des AS, Paris
Association de Veielles Tiges, Paris
Federation of French War Veterans, Los Angeles, USA
Forsvarets Overkommando, Luftforsvarsstaben, Oslo, Norway
Ministry of Defence RAF Personnel Management Centre, Gloucester, UK
Des Salons Internabonalaux de l'Aéronautique et de L'Espace, Paris

Individuals (General)

Arnold, Peter R. (Newport Pagnell, UK)
Cooke, Peter (Reading, UK)
Evans, Mike (Rolls-Royce Ltd, Derby)
Grace, Carolyn (Essex, UK)
Grace, Nick (late, Chichester, UK)
Henshaw, Alex (Bury St Edmunds, UK)
Jameson, Paul (late, Shoreham, UK)
Krepski, Ludwik (Reading, UK)
Melchers, Theo (Onderkerk aan de Amstel, Netherlands)
Mulelly, Ian (Uxbridge, UK)
Scrope, Hugh (London, UK)
Szelewski (Rickmansworth, UK)
van der Meer, Harry (Hoffddorp, Netherlands)

ATA

Curtis, Lettice (Reading, UK)
Moggridge, Jackie (Taunton, UK)

485 Squadron

Bongard, Ernie (Henderson, NZ)
Clarke, Doug DFC, AFC, C de G (Auckland, NZ)
Clarke, Russ DFC (Hamilton, NZ)
Collett, Max (Napier, NZ)
Downer, Athol (late, Auckland, NZ)
Edwards, Derek (Crowborough, UK)
Gardiner, Mrs Louisa (Wakatipu, NZ)
Hardy, Owen DFC & bar, AFC (Chichester, UK)
Houlton, Johnnie DFC (Wellsford, NZ)
Humphrey, Peter (Rotorua, NZ)
Hunt, C.J. (late, Farnham Common, UK)
Jordon, Len (Rode, UK)

King, J. Norby (Papamoa, NZ)
Lee, Ken DFC (Auckland, NZ)
Macdonald, Keith DFC (Cambridge, NZ)
Mayston, Maurice (Lower Hutt, NZ)
Mechan, Philip (Brighton, UK)
Norman, Richard (late, Plymouth, UK)
Patterson, Mrs I.B. (Wairarapa, NZ)
Platten, Edgar (Great Yarmouth, UK)
Roberts, Allan (Christchurch, NZ)
Roddis, Joe (Derby, UK)
Strange, Vic (Brentwood, UK)
Transom, Frank (Tai Hape, NZ)
Wheal, Ken (Pershore, UK)
White, L.S.M. (late, Ruatoria, NZ)
White, Ron (Faversham, UK)
White, S. (formerly Bradley, Halstead, UK)
Wilson, Stan (Bowdon, UK)

341 Squadron

Alépée, Claude (late, Marseille, France)
Christinacce, G. (Reading, UK)
Dabos, Johnny (Grau du Roi, France)
Duperier Bernard (Paris, France)
Michel, Maurice (Villeneuve Les Angnon, France)

308 Squadron

Mierzejewski, J. (late, Great Chesterford, UK)
Sawoszczyk, Jozef KW & 2 bars (Jersey City, USA)
Stanski, Waclaw VM, DFC, KW & 2 bars (late, Plok, Poland)
Witkowski, J. (Trentham, UK)

349 Squadron

Banks, Alan (Saffron Walden, U.K)
Branders, Léon (Bruxelles, Belgium)
Seydel, Gaby DFC (late, Stoke on Trent, UK)
Van Hamme, Albert (Malmédy, Belgium)

345 Squadron

Accart, Général (late, Paris)
Boyer de Bouillane, Felix (Paris)
Droumatakis, Georges (Marseille, France)
Le Boëtté, René (Versailles, France)
Harmel, Léon, (Los Angeles, USA)
Guizard, Mme J. (Paris)
Perdrizet, Général M. (Crest, France)
Perseval, General G. (Locmine, France)
Pierquet, C.A. (Quincy Voisins, France)
Vaisse, Claude (Montauroux, France)

332 Squadron

Anonsen, Ronald (Cleveland, USA)

Christie, Werner (Oslo, Norway)
Roesland, Johannes (Gjettum, Norway)
Stigset, Egil (late, Algarheim, Norway)

151 RU(A)

Thorn, Jack (late, Cardiff, UK)
Pickering, James (Hinckley, UK)

Irish Air Corps

Ferguson, Capt E. (Ireland)
Healy, Tim (Dublin, Ireland)
Howard, Henry (Dublin, Ireland)
Kearns, Anthony P. (Dublin, Ireland)
McCarron, Donald (Gerrards Cross, UK)
Moore, Lt Col J. (Dublin, Ireland)
O'Malley, Lt Col, M. (Dublin, Ireland)
Skillen, Graham (Tonbridge, UK)
Sweeney, Charles (Dublin, Ireland)
Waring, Stewart (Grantham, UK)